Building Your IR Theory Toolbox

An Introduction to Understanding World Politics

EDITED BY

ERIC K. LEONARD

SHENANDOAH UNIVERSITY

ROWMAN & LITTLEFIELD

Lanham • Boulder • New York • London

Executive Editor: Traci Crowell
Assistant Editor: Mary Malley
Senior Marketing Manager: Kim Lyons

Credits and acknowledgments for material borrowed from other sources, and reproduced with permission, appear on the appropriate page within the text.

Published by Rowman & Littlefield
A wholly owned subsidiary of The Rowman & Littlefield Publishing Group, Inc.
4501 Forbes Boulevard, Suite 200, Lanham, Maryland 20706
www.rowman.com

Unit A, Whitacre Mews, 26-34 Stannary Street, London SE11 4AB, United Kingdom

Copyright © 2018 by Rowman & Littlefield

British Library Cataloguing in Publication Information Available

Library of Congress Cataloging-in-Publication Data
Names: Leonard, Eric K.
Title: Building your IR theory toolbox : an introduction to understanding
    world politics / edited by Eric K. Leonard, Shenandoah University.
Description: Lanham, Maryland : Rowman & Littlefield, [2018] | Includes
    bibliographical references and index.
Identifiers: LCCN 2017060478 (print) | LCCN 2018000901 (ebook) | ISBN
    9780742567443 (electronic) | ISBN 9780742567429 (cloth : alk. paper) |
    ISBN 9780742567436 (pbk. : alk. paper)
Subjects: LCSH: International relations—Philosophy. | World politics.
Classification: LCC JZ1305 (ebook) | LCC JZ1305.B85 2018 (print) | DDC
    327.101—dc23
LC record available at https://lccn.loc.gov/2017060478

♾™ The paper used in this publication meets the minimum requirements of American National Standard for Information Sciences—Permanence of Paper for Printed Library Materials, ANSI/NISO Z39.48-1992.

Printed in the United States of America

Dedication

This book is dedicated to my wife, Lisa Mennella.
Whenever I doubt my abilities or my place in
this profession, you provide the encouragement
and support I need. For that I am eternally grateful.

Contents

Preface

The creation of this book took a long and winding path. However, the one thing that continuously drove the project was my desire to make International Relations (IR) theory accessible to the typical undergraduate student. In many ways, this passion emerged from my own journey to academia. Upon finally going to college for an education and not for the plethora of other reasons that existed, I landed at a mid-sized state school in New Jersey. Prior to this point, I was not the best student, nor the most attentive, but at William Paterson College I found professors who cared about my future and believed in my potential. These professors understood their students' background and their struggles, yet continued to push them academically, but in a way that remained accessible. As a result of this education, when I began teaching almost twenty years ago it was with the same mindset as those that had educated me during my undergraduate years. I entered academia to teach first and research second. My goal was to gain employment at a teaching-oriented institution where I could help undergraduates develop academically.

And this brings me back to this book. In many ways, this book is the embodiment of what I wanted to bring to academia. For years I heard many professors at teaching-oriented institutions talk about the struggles of teaching IR theory in their intro-level class. They talked about the inability of students to understand theory, the lack of interest by the many non-political science students in their class to engage theory, and the lack of literature written for their student population. I can fully attest to the fact that this struggle was real. For a stretch of several years I toyed with the idea of eliminating or at least minimizing the theory section of my intro class. However, if the goal of my class was to help students understand the world around them, then theory was necessary.

The other problem was the shortened theory sections that were now a standard in the introductory textbooks. Many of the authors of these textbooks were providing one to two pages on each theory, only providing an overview of the key concepts with no real depth to the discussion. This was only pushing the discipline towards the problem discussed above, minimizing or in some cases eliminating theory from the introductory course.

It was only after articulating these issues to Rowman & Littlefield editor Susan McEachern that the idea of correcting this problem began to take shape. Susan McEachern's encouragement pushed me to consider this textbook as a way to bring theory back into the typical undergraduate classroom in a way that students could both understand and apply. I can only hope that this small book provides a means for instructors to bring theory back into the Introduction to International Politics classroom so that all students can gain access to the academic tools that will assist them in understanding the world around them.

Acknowledgments

This book would not have been possible without the constant support and assistance of Rowman & Littlefield's vice president and senior acquisition editor Susan McEachern. This book emerged from a conversation with Susan at the annual International Studies Association conference far too many years ago. Despite the length of time since that initial meeting and the many delays in this project, Susan kept encouraging me to complete the project and provided unending support and feedback. For that support I am truly grateful. Along the same lines, I am grateful to all of the contributors to this textbook for their willingness to stay with the project and provide a wonderful resource for the students of IR theory. Alice Ba, Matthew Hoffmann, Mark Sachleben, Rose Shinko, and Laura Sjoberg were wonderful colleagues and contributors throughout this process, and I thank them for their unending patience. This book also benefited greatly from the comments, insights, and criticisms of the following reviewers: Christopher Cook, Bob Denemark, Rebeccah Evans, Michael Jacobs, Brian Klunk, Jyotika Saksena, Gregory Williams, and Jeremy Youde. I would be remiss if I failed to thank my students at Shenandoah University. In many ways this project is about those students and my desire to make IR theory accessible to them. I employed many earlier drafts in my Introduction to International Politics class and I thank my students for their insights on how to improve each chapter. I also owe a tremendous debt to my institution, Shenandoah University. The course release time, sabbatical, and several faculty development grants SU awarded me were critical pieces to completing this project. Also, the institution's encouragement to improve my teaching and the acknowledgment that the drafting of a textbook would assist in that process were fundamental parts of a successful completion of this manuscript. Finally, I would like to thank my wife, Lisa Mennella, and my three kids, Nico, Stefani, and Mathieu. They provided an emotional support throughout this process that simply cannot be measured. Thank you for always being there for me, even when the struggles of writing made me irritable.

CHAPTER 1

Introduction

Helping You Understand the World

Eric K. Leonard

Welcome to your introduction to International Relations (IR) theory.[1] These very words have struck fear in many an undergraduate student. The thought of theory, with a basis in philosophy (even scarier), is to many students neither exciting nor engaging. In fact, it may be something that you would expect belongs in a more advanced International Politics class rather than a 100- or 200-level survey class. In this class, you were probably expecting to discuss and debate current events—like whether terrorism is still a major threat to global security or whether Iran having a nuclear weapon threatens global stability or why the distribution of wealth in the global economy is so unequal or how do states work to control global climate change. I am sure you anticipated that these topics, and many more, would be the focus of the conversation and content of the course, and I do not doubt that these types of conversations will be a fundamental part of the class. However, in order to understand these topics, you need more than just facts—you need theory!

When discussing one of the aforementioned topics, or any current event in world politics, students must ask themselves what they are trying to gain from the discussion. Are you simply trying to gain knowledge about the facts of the case so that someday you can win at a Trivial Pursuit game? Or do you want to gain an understanding of the topic and how it affects not only the world around you but you as well? As students of international politics, you should be able to understand the world and the political entities that make up that world. I know that in my introductory classes if at the end of the semester students feel that they can listen to and understand a National Public Radio (NPR) news report or read a *New York Times* article on something global-oriented, I have done my job. I remember one fall semester when a student of mine returned from Thanksgiving break and proudly exclaimed that on the ride home from campus her father was listening to a story on NPR about the United Nations, and she was able not only to understand the topic but also to explain parts of it to her father. In my Introduction to International Politics class, that is evidence that the course has accomplished its primary learning objective.

But fulfilling this very simple objective entails more than just knowing about the United Nations or whatever organization oversees global trade; it entails understanding why states, intergovernmental organizations (IGOs), nongovernmental organizations (NGOs), multinational corporations (MNCs), terrorist organizations, or any other global actors behave the way they do and why they interact with other organizations/actors the way they do. In the end, only theory can help with this objective.

What Is Theory?

The place to start is with some understanding of theory itself. As with many concepts you will hear throughout this semester, theory is a term that you all recognize and know but no one has ever asked you to define it. So what does this very important term mean? Basically, theory is a means by which one answers questions. Chris Brown and Kirsten Ainley put it best when they stated, "We turn to theory when the answer to a question that is, for one reason or another, important to us is not clear."[2] Thus, theory is best defined as a set of linked propositions and/ or concepts that provide an improved description and understanding of a particular phenomenon. If you apply this term to the field of world politics, we see that theory is used to explain and understand why states, NGOs, IGOs, terrorist organizations, MNCs, etc., behave the way they do. It helps clarify the world around you and makes some sense of the mess that is world politics.

The way IR theory does this is by generating hypotheses (basically a good guess at why things occur) and then testing those hypotheses. Now the testing of hypotheses to create theory is the part that remains contestable in the study of world politics. The problem is what constitutes a good test. The typical response is that empirical data must be the basis for any hypothesis. What we mean by empirical is tangible information or things that you can see, touch, or sense. An empirical analysis is grounded in things that you can "prove" or at least provide evidence of their existence. And although all theories agree that empirical analysis is the basis for generating a good hypothesis and theory, they do not all agree on what they see. As I will discuss below, not all theories see the same thing in the world and claiming that what you see is "truth" is always contestable because not everyone sees things the same way. Nevertheless, relying on some sense of empirical analysis at least gets us closer to some testable hypotheses and stronger theory.

As stated above, theory is primarily about describing and understanding (often referred to as explaining) what is going on in the world, but its purpose goes beyond these attributes. The other thing theory is supposed to do is predict. This is the point where theory can carry over from the academic world to the policy world. What every theory is going to do is provide what it believes is the best description and understanding of the world, and how the actors in that world behave. However, once this is complete, there is the possibility to predict future behavior. For instance, if I have a theory on student behavior based on empirical data (what I see on a daily basis), it might tell me that in introductory classes (possibly like the one you are sitting in right now), students tend not to read the textbook. I base this hypothesis on years and years of teaching and experience and conclude that most students in an Intro to International Politics class will not read the textbook. This provides me predictive capabilities for how my students in the following semester are going to behave and allows me to make policy to try to affect that behavior. Maybe I really want students to read, but I predict that they won't. As a result, I might build daily quizzes into my syllabus to alter their behavior patterns. This is where you can use theory to create policy, and it is no different in the realm of foreign policy. Now do not confuse this class with your foreign policy class—I do not believe you will be creating policy in this class. However, it is important that you see the overlap between the two fields and understand that the predictive capabilities of IR theory provide for that overlap.

It is also important to realize that not all IR theories put the same emphasis on predictive capabilities. In fact, some of the theories you will engage with in this semester feel that prediction of actor behavior is difficult, if not impossible. However, this does not discount them as IR theory, and it should not push you to ignore those theories. In essence, what theories like social constructivism and postmodernism argue is that the world is more complex than some of the more traditional theories, like realism and liberalism, would want you to believe. Predicting behavior patterns is not simple or easy, and understanding behavior is a complex process that needs to be unpacked at multiple levels. In the end, you may find that these complex theories add as much or more to your toolbox, despite their dismissiveness of prediction.

Building My Toolbox

In looking at the theoretical landscape of world politics, things can be a bit overwhelming. It seems that there are so many theories and not enough time. In many ways, it is helpful to create a bit of a roadmap for our tour of IR theory or a short primer on where your study of IR theory will take you.

The place to begin is with the first debate of IR theory. This debate took place during the interwar period (the 1920s and 1930s) and focused on the question of why World War I occurred, and how, if at all, the global community could avoid a future world war. The two opposing perspectives in this early debate were the classical realists and the classical liberals. As you will see in the respective chapters on these theories, they had two very different viewpoints on the world. However, let us simplify things a bit and state that the classical realists believe that war is an almost inevitable occurrence in world politics, while the classical liberals believed it was avoidable. Can you guess who won this debate? Well, you only need to know what happened to end the interwar period to understand who won the debate and why. With the onset of World War II, the classical realist appeared to have a much better explanatory and predictive tool at their disposal, while the classical liberals seemed wholly out of touch with the empirical world around them. Notice that I say *seemed* wholly out of touch, because how quickly things can change in the realm of world politics!

Although the classical realists won out in this initial debate, neither theory remained stagnant. Both evolved over the decades to create new and improved versions of these classical perspectives. For the realists this "improvement" occurred in 1979 with the publication of Kenneth Waltz's *Theory of International Politics*. Waltz's new version of realism became known as structural realism or neorealism, for reasons that you will discover in chapter 2. The lineage of liberalism is not as simple. After "losing" in the first debate, the liberals had to rethink their approach to understanding world politics. The coming decades meant a progression of thought that takes students from functionalism (1950s), to complex interdependence (1977), and finally to neoliberal institutionalism (1982). One of the more interesting aspects of the culminating neoliberal model is that it borrows from the enemy—using many neorealist attributes to understand the large amount of cooperation occurring in the world. It is the debate between these two "mainstream" theories (as they came to be known) that students must engage first.

Aside from the mainstream theories, lots of other perspectives on how to understand world politics emerged over the decades. Students will engage four of the more prominent challengers from this set of "alternative" theories—Marxist theory, social constructivism, feminist theory, and postmodernism. All of these theories view world politics from a less than widely accepted point of view; therefore, it is fair to say that they have not had the same impact on the study of world politics as the realists and liberals (at least not to date, although that could certainly change). However, this does not mean that they do not have interesting, important, and influential things to say about our world and how we study it. In many ways, what they say may be more interesting and engaging because they want to think outside of the mainstream theories. The alternative perspectives are typically more interesting—that is why they are the more alternative. So as an introduction to these sections, I would simply say, read and enjoy! Also, be sure to open your mind to some opposing perspectives. If you allow these theories to wash over you, you might be surprised to see how influential they can be to your worldview, and how important they are to understanding the complex world around you.

One thing that students should be aware of is that the theories discussed in this text are quite complex. Therefore, although each chapter provides a clear and fairly robust dialogue about each theory, the intent is not to deliver a full overview of each theory and all of its possible offshoots. For example, when discussing realism, the focus remains on classical realism and structural realism. Other forms of realism exist, such as offensive realism, defensive realism, and others, but for the purpose of an introductory class, it is important to provide a basic understanding of the main theoretical attributes of each theory and not get bogged down in all the subsidiary debates that exist within those theories. In the end, there are always more theoretical perspectives to discover, but without a solid grounding in the primary attributes, understanding those other perspectives is not possible.

Is There a Right Answer?

The preceding section of this introduction set up the book as if it were a competition among theories. I used terms like enemy, lost, mainstream, and alternative, and for many students of world politics, it is a competition. From the perspective of your instructor, I bet he/she wishes there was a right answer and a clear-cut winner in this competition. Moreover, not just a right answer but also an answer that those who study world politics could all agree is accurate. The reason for such wishful thinking is the simplicity of having just one answer to how the world works. Think about how easy this class, and most likely the study of world politics, would be if there was one theory that explained, understood, and predicted the future of world affairs. Instructors could simply walk in the first day of class, state that realism (since for so long it was the most widely accepted theory) was correct, proceed to teach realism and ONLY realism, and then spend the rest of the semester applying this theory to our perfect understanding of the world around us. Your description of the world would be flawless, your understanding perfect, and your predictive capabilities spot on.

Unfortunately, or possibly fortunately, that is not how IR theory works. As I just explained, IR theory is diverse with several different understandings of not only how actors behave but also who the primary influential actors are in the global system. Having such contestation in the study of world politics does make things difficult, but it also makes things interesting. I stated that the diversity of theory might be a fortunate attribute of the field, and that is because things never stay the same. Nothing is static in the study of world politics; everything is constantly changing; and the debate over how to understand the world around us is always raging—and this is a good thing! You can never claim that the study of world politics is not interesting, and there always seems to be a new way to view the world around us.

Nevertheless, can diversity be problematic? Many IR scholars believe it is. Those individuals view IR theory as a competition for supremacy in explaining and understanding the world around us. However, this book approaches diversity not as a problem, but as a good thing. The class that requires you to read this book may be about the study of world politics, but at its core, it is about the study of politics—just on a global scale. Politics by its very nature is not definable in hard science, empirical terms. It is a social science—something that we may want to emulate the hard sciences (like biology and chemistry) but is never truly capable of achieving this status. What is the primary reason for this lack of empirical, objective, and defensible data? People! The study of politics is the study of people and human behavior. The moment that human behavior becomes completely predictable is the moment that IR scholars can apply the laws of political science. Until that moment, and I think we will be waiting quite some time for that moment, the study of politics will remain somewhat unpredictable.

So, what does this mean for theory? I am sure it is quite confusing at this point, because I stated earlier that theory is supposed to describe, understand, and predict. In the natural sciences, scholars accept diversity (or theoretical pluralism) because it will eventually reach some sort of consensus. This idea of "unity over the horizon" is not something that appears attainable in the study of world politics.[3] So where does this leave IR theory and its large number of theories? It leaves us in the wonderful position of embracing the notion of theoretical pluralism and engaging the ensuing debates—but that idea of engagement is the key. Tim Dunne, Lene Hansen, and Colin Wight put it clearly when they discuss the idea of integrative pluralism, not disengaged pluralism.[4] Disengaged pluralism embraces the idea that theoretical pluralism exists but that the alternative theories will not engage or speak to one another. Thus, it is an interesting means of gaining knowledge, but it looks a whole lot like the U.S. Congress where no one listens to each other, everyone talks past one another, and nothing gets done. Integrative pluralism, on the other hand, involves a discussion amongst the diverse theoretical perspectives. We can view this approach as a dialogue to assist scholars and students of world politics in their accurate description and understanding of our world, and to some degree also in their predictive capability concerning what the world might become.

What this means for you, as students of world politics, is that this book is not a competition for the best theory or the most accurate theory. It is a book to assist you in describing the world you live in, understanding those massive events that people on NPR and in the *New York Times* and other scary news outlets discuss, and possibly gaining some predictive capability about what will happen next time a similar event arises. All of the theories in this textbook are your tools for accomplishing this goal. Without the right tools, one cannot fulfill the goal. Try painting your walls without a paintbrush, or digging a ditch without a shovel, or hanging a picture without a hammer. Maybe you could do it, but it is going to be really hard. Tools help you accomplish goals and objectives. If your objective in this class is to understand the world around you, then IR theory is the tool to help you attain that objective. Good luck in your journey!

Wrap-Up

The end of every chapter includes a wrap-up section and list of resources for future readings. The wrap-up session is simply supposed to provide you with a few key take-home ideas or concepts. For this chapter, here is the take-home message: IR theory is an essential part of studying world politics. Without theory, you are basically engaged in a current events' class, not an academic study of the world. Thus, this book becomes a foundational part of your knowledge and understanding of world politics. Theory should also provide you with the ability to describe the world and the actors' behaviors accurately, understand why those actors behave in that manner, and predict how they might behave in the future. Finally, IR theory is diverse, but that is not necessarily a bad thing. As you read this book, be sure to engage in the dialogue among the theories and see how the application of all the "tools" to study world politics helps you better understand the world around you.

Further Reading

1. Tim Dunne, Milja Kurki, and Steve Smith, eds. *International Relations Theories: Discipline and Diversity* (2013), is a more detailed engagement of many of the theories discussed in this textbook, along with some that are not. The chapter on critical theory is an excellent addition to the theories discussed in this text, along with chapters on the English School, Postcolonialism, and Green Theory.
2. Patrick Thaddeus Jackson, "What Is Theory?" (2010), is an outstanding introduction to the role of theory in the study of world politics. For any student wishing to engage theoretical understandings of world politics, this article is an excellent starting point due to its breadth of analysis and thorough engagement of the literature.
3. David A. Lake, "Theory Is Dead, Long Live Theory: The End of the Great Debates and the Rise of Eclecticism in International Relations" (2013), provides students with an excellent discussion of theoretical pluralism. As discussed in this chapter, theoretical arguments/debates are a part of the discipline, but Lake provides a defensible argument for moving beyond these debates as a way to gain a better understanding of the world around us.
4. Paul R. Viotti and Mark V. Kauppi, *International Relations Theory: Realism, Pluralism, Globalism, and Beyond* (2012), is another detailed and advanced engagement of IR theory. For many this remains the seminal survey text on IR theory and an excellent resource for students who wish to learn more about theory and its application.

Notes

[1] "International Relations" is the traditional way scholars refer to the field and IR theory is how they reference the primary subject of this textbook. However, you should be aware that many scholars refer to this field of study as International Politics or even Global Politics. I would ask that you do not get hung up on the terms and simply understand that for the purpose of this introductory textbook these terms are interchangeable.

[2] Chris Brown and Kirsten Ainley, *Understanding International Relations*, 3rd edition (New York, NY: Palgrave/Macmillan, 2005), 7–8.

³ This phrase comes from Tim Dunne and a wonderful blog discussion on the idea of theoretical pluralism, http://www.whiteoliphaunt.com/duckofminerva/2013/09/the-end-of-international-relations-theory.html. For those looking to engage this topic in greater detail, I would suggest looking at the special issue of *The European Journal of International Relations*, cited below.

⁴ Tim Dunne, Lene Hansen, and Colin Wight, "The End of International Relations Theory," *The European Journal of International Relations* 19, no. 3 (2013): 415–17.

Works Cited

Brown, Chris, and Kirsten Ainley. 2005. *Understanding International Relations*, 3rd edition. New York: Palgrave/Macmillan, 7–8.

Dunne, Tim, Lene Hansen, and Colin Wight. 2013. "The End of International Relations Theory." *The European Journal of International Relations*. 19, no. 3: 415–25.

Dunne, Tim, Milja Kurki, and Steve Smith, eds. 2013. *International Relations Theories: Discipline and Diversity*. Oxford: Oxford University Press.

Lake, David A. 2013. "Theory Is Dead, Long Live Theory: The End of the Great Debates and the Rise of Eclecticism in International Relations." *European Journal of International Relations*. 19, no. 3: 567–87.

Nexon, Daniel, ed. 2013. "Symposium—End of International Relations Theory?" *The European Journal of International Relations*. 19, no. 3.

Jackson, Patrick Thaddeus. 2010. "What is theory?". http://www.isacompendium.com/subscriber/tocnode?d=g9781444336597_chunk_g978144433659721_ss1–5.

Viotti, Paul R., and Mark V. Kauppi. 2012. *International Relations Theory: Realism, Pluralism, Globalism, and Beyond*, 5th edition. Boston, MA: Longman.

CHAPTER 2

Realism and Neorealism

Power-Based Theory

Mark Sachleben

The realists emerged during the interwar period in an attempt to explain the causes of World War I and the ensuing international system. It is in their first debate with the liberals (discussed further in the following chapter) that we get the foundational ideas of IR theory. However, this theory is not something new to the early twentieth century. Realism, as a perspective on politics, is grounded in some of the great political thinkers of the Western world, including Thucydides, Augustine, Niccoló Machiavelli, and Thomas Hobbes. It is these philosophers' stark, empirical understanding of politics that serves as the foundation for one of the most widely accepted theories in world politics.

The world is complex and seemingly difficult to explain. Events and movements create the impression of a world of change and stability. The world of fifty, one hundred, or even three hundred years ago is very different from the world of today. Or is it? Realism, and its modern variant neorealism (or structural realism), seeks to give us a short, easy explanation of world politics—one that focuses on how international politics has basically been the same throughout human history. The realist explanation tries to cut through issues that are not as important as one might think in order to help decipher the behavior of states on the world stage.

World politics is, according to realism, incredibly easy to explain. That is because there is one concept, a single resource, which consistently permeates all politics, regardless of time or place: power! Realists argue that you can understand and explain world politics by simply understanding why people want power, who has power, and how power is distributed. However, it is not simply the lust for power for power's sake that explains politics. Realists base their assumptions on the idea that humans are flawed and insecure beings that are constantly seeking to fulfill their self-interest. The best and most direct way to provide for their security (which is the most fundamental of self-interests) is through the acquisition of power.

One of the primary claims of realism is that it attempts to explain what the world actually looks like, not what it should be. Thus, the utility of the realist perspective is to strip away the baggage of what we want to happen (the normative explanations) and explain what is actually happening (the empirical reality). From this perspective, realism is cold, hard, and uncompromising. It has a reputation as being bleak and hopeless; however, for those advocates of the perspective, realism offers a clinical approach to world politics that is useful in describing, understanding, and predicting.

Thinking Like a Realist

Have you ever noticed that when you walk down a beach or are in a bar, there are guys around that wear tank-tops that show off their muscles? What message are they sending out? Basically that they have muscles (weapons) that are so powerful that you do not want to mess with them. Simply put, they can take care of themselves. States do the same thing; they hold military parades of their latest technology, soldiers marching in rigid formation, and highlight their successes in effect saying, "We are so powerful that it would be a mistake to try to fight us." States are trying to demonstrate their power in an attempt to deter an attack from others, the same as our muscle-bound friends on the beach or in the bar.

However, one must also ask whether humans are all essentially the same, regardless of time, culture, or place? Do people, at the most basic level, seek the same thing? According to the realists, humans want physical security. After they achieve security, they might want other things, but they cannot pursue the "other things" until they are secure. Think about your own life—when you go to sleep at night, what do you do? Lock the door. Why? To ascertain some sense of security. Some people will own a gun and keep it accessible in their house or possibly even have a license to carry that weapon. Again, the rationale is a sense of security. In general, so much of what we do as human beings is in an attempt to ascertain security. Humans construct societies, institutions, and live to pursue one thing: security. Without security, humans can get nothing else done. And the sure way to get security is through power. The more power accumulated, the more secure we are. Realists argue that states are no different from humans. They exist to provide security for their population and territory. Therefore, states are obsessed with power because through power one can achieve security.

Foundational Principles

Although realism has several different iterations, including classical realism and structural realism, at its core they all share a common set of five principles that help us understand the world and how to interpret it.[1] Although these concepts are listed as distinct characteristics, it is important to recognize that they all relate to one another to create the system of world politics that realists believe is empirically accurate.

First, the primary phenomenon a realist studies in politics, including world politics, is power. All political units are seeking power, and thus their interests lie in the accumulation of power. The primary reason for this desire is that power is a way to guarantee security (a theme we will return to shortly), and without power, a state is vulnerable. This emphasis on power permeates all other aspects of realism, regardless of what iteration of realism you are studying. Hans Morgenthau captured this best when he stated, "International politics, like all politics, is a struggle for power."[2] Thus, when analyzing a decision, realists always ask, "How will this affect the power of the state?"[3]

Second, the current international system is based upon the idea that states are the primary actors and that states hold sovereignty, meaning they have exclusive jurisdiction over their own territory.[4] In other words, states, which are commonly referred to as countries or nations, are the actor that has the right to exercise decision-making authority in world politics. This exclusive jurisdiction means that, at least in theory, no one outside of the state can tell the state how to run its own affairs. Theoretically, both China (with 1.3 billion people) and the Bahamas (with three hundred thousand people) have the same rights and can expect to be free from outside influence. At the same time, both states have the responsibility to make sure that what occurs on their territories does not adversely affect other members of the international system.

The third is the realist emphasis on a Hobbesian conception of human nature.[5] According to the great political philosopher Thomas Hobbes, human beings are naturally appetitive, desirous entities whose primary goal is to fulfill their appetite (desires) and avoid their aversions (fears). This creates a situation where humanity is prone to corruption, greed, and insecurity. If discussed within the realm of international politics, this creates a condition where states are in a constant state of competition to fulfill their self-interest, and this often results in insecurity and conflict. Taking this understanding of human nature one-step further, we can link this to the first foundational principle in that the best way to fulfill one's self-interest is to gain more power than everyone else has. Thus, the system becomes a constant state of competition for relative power. The goal is simply to fulfill your self-interest by whatever means necessary.

As the Prussian King Fredrick the Great observed, "If we gain something by being honest, we will be it, and if we have to deceive, we will be cheats."[6]

Fourth, the international system is anarchical. Anarchy is the situation in which there is no centralized government. Many people would associate anarchy with chaos; however, this is not always the case. Actually, in the case of the international system, anarchy can be very orderly and many things happen on a routine basis. Nevertheless, for a realist, the phenomenon of anarchy is very important to the understanding of world politics because if coupled with the previous principles, it provides a context of self-help. In other words, if a state wishes to fulfill their self-interest or a state is attacked in an anarchical system, who can they call for help? No one. Counterpoise this with a hierarchical domestic system like the United States, where if someone attacks a citizen, that victim can simply call the police for assistance. However, in an anarchical system that enforcement of laws simply does not exist. The result is a situation where appetitive and desirous states, without recourse to a centralized authority, are in a constant state of competition for relative power. If we follow the Hobbesian logic, the resulting system is conflict-ridden and insecure or, as Hobbes described it, "a war of all against all."[7]

Finally, there is an understanding that there is a moral significance to political action; however, there is a difference between *understanding* the moral difference and being *guided* by it.[8] Realism assumes that an emphasis on moral issues hides the true motivation of political actions, which we now know is a desire for power. Closely related is the notion that realism does not identify the moral aspiration of a single state with the moral laws that govern the universe. In fact, realists do not believe that one set of moral laws exists in the international system. Thus, to assume that a single state holds the key to human conscience is a conceit. As stated earlier, realism seeks to understand what is observably true from what we want to be true (the empirical from the normative). As a result, realism recognizes that all states are tempted to disguise their actions as benefiting a universal moral purpose, when in fact it is benefiting the individual state and its interests. In the end, morality is not a determining factor for state behavior. States behave in an amoral manner because there is an inability of the international community to rely on a universal sense of morality.

Now that we have a basic understanding of realism and its primary principles, let's see if we can't clarify the image of realist behavior patterns with a simple, non-international politics scenario. Imagine a town in which two neighbors (John and Sally) live with their families.

The town is anarchical (lacking centralized authority)—there is no mayor, no police, and no fire department. John and Sally must depend on themselves to provide protection for their families and property. Sally and her family love dogs, and they own a pair of German shepherds as family pets. Sally owns these dogs not only because of her love of dogs but also because they provide a certain measure of protection from unwanted intruders. John, Sally's neighbor, must pay attention to Sally's behavior because no one else will. Remember, there is no centralized authority in this community. In John's eyes, Sally's German shepherds might pose a threat to younger or elderly members of his household. As a result, he considers building a fence to ensure the safety of his family. The selection of such a fence is very important: little hands and dogs' muscles can get through chain-link fences, and an active dog can easily jump a short fence. Thus, John chooses to build a six-foot-high brick fence that will protect his family. According to John, the fence is designed to protect his family, not to antagonize Sally. But Sally finds herself in a similar situation—she must provide for the safety of her family. This means she must be vigilant in seeking their security. The dogs help, but it is hardly sufficient. She must keep track of everything and everyone, worrying about where potential threats to her and her family's security might come. She must do this because no one else will do it for her. In an anarchical system, it is a self-help system. Also, remember that Sally and John are both trying to fulfill their self-interest, which in this case entails security of themselves, their family, and their property.

As a result, Sally looks at that brick fence and wonders what John and his family are doing behind it. It could be nothing, but on the other hand, he might be making plans to do her and her family harm. It is a reasonable and sensible precaution to make sure that John plans no harm through the observation of his property. Sally could accomplish this goal either surreptitiously (spying) or through direct observation (security cameras). If John is planning something nefarious, there is no one to call (no police, no judge), and Sally must be prepared for any eventuality. Nevertheless, John is likely to be unhappy with the attention and as a result, he will respond in kind. This seems to be a reasonable response since he too must be concerned with the safety of his family. But any such reaction from John will probably be viewed by Sally as confirmation of her worst fears—John is paying attention, and her safety might well be at risk. At the end of the day, Sally and John must be preoccupied with their own security because if they are not, no one else will be.

Notice that the above scenario, while pushed along for the sake of brevity, is a result of anarchy and the self-interested nature of the characters. John and Sally's intentions might not be nefarious at all;

however, the result of their insecurities and their efforts to address their insecurities is the insecurity of those around them. In world politics, this scenario is known as the *security dilemma*. IR scholars define a security dilemma as the situation in which in anarchy, the measures one state takes to feel more secure inevitably leads to other states feeling less secure. For all realists, the fundamental characteristic of the international system is that the world is anarchical because anarchy drives states to seek power to satisfy their insecurity, which remains their number one self-interest.

Classical Realism

Most American political scientists look to Hans Morgenthau as the father of modern realism. In his seminal work, *Politics among Nations: The Struggle for Peace and Power*, originally published in 1948, Morgenthau laid out the basic principles upon which the perspective was founded. In this text, Morgenthau tried to capture how world politics could be explained by a systematic understanding of it that did not get caught up in *what should be* but focused on *what is* and attempted to derive policies based on how different actors might understand their interests. This "realistic" view of the world first finds voice in E. H. Carr's classic text, *The Twenty Years' Crisis*. In this text, Carr takes on the classical liberal argument that war can be avoided via educated leadership and collective security (discussed at length in the next chapter). According to Carr, the liberal or idealist (as he referred to it) perspective is utopian and lacks any empirical validity. In this first debate, Carr argues that the idea of a harmony of interests existing among international states is simply false and that any notion of universal interests or universal morality is simply each state defining what they believe would be best for the international system. Morgenthau picks up on this view of the world and expands upon it to give us a more detailed understanding of what realism looks like in IR theory.

Morgenthau's view of classical realism relies heavily on the Hobbesian conception of human nature and its impact on state behavior, despite the fact that he cites Hobbes only once in a footnote. As he states in his seminal work, "Political realism believes that politics, like society in general, is governed by objective laws that have their roots in human nature."[9] This basic conceptualization establishes two key principles of classical realism: (a) that realism is empirical and not normative or subjective and (b) that an empirical understanding of human nature provides the best explanation of state behavior. Therefore, what we see with classical realism is an understanding of state behavior that is fixed or static. States behave in a way that promotes their desires or appetites and avoids their fears or aversions. As a result, when placed into the anarchical nature of the international system, it becomes apparent to statesmen that the best way to ascertain your interest is to gain more power than others do. Power, according to Morgenthau, provides you a means of securing your national interest and protecting your citizenry, and states should act in whatever way is needed to secure their national interest. In other words, morality is not a defining cause of state behavior. The result is a self-help system in which states are constantly seeking power. Thus, the prospects for war and conflict become evident. This conflict-ridden system is not something that realists want or take pride in espousing; it is simply the empirical reality and the most accurate description of world politics.

A critique of this early form of realism was that the world was not as Morgenthau described because, in his text, he was offering advice to foreign policy makers rather than an academic judgment about the construct of the international system. Thus, policy makers were behaving in terms of moral imperatives and public preferences, rather than as realists predicted. Further, it was a natural American belief that states could avoid war and that war was not natural. Most Americans believed that their country was highly moral, and even morally superior to other countries. Therefore, American foreign policy had to be moral as well.[10] Many realists argued that classical realism had the world right, but it failed to provide testable evidence that rhetorical justifications hid policy makers' true intent.[11] The attempt to correct this empirical accuracy and other critiques of classical realism comes in the form of structural realism.

Structural Realism (or Neorealism)

Kenneth Waltz's 1979 text, *Theory of International Politics,* was a seminal moment in IR theory. It is with this publication that realism addresses many of the previously unanswered questions and moves IR theory toward a more "scientific" study of world politics. Waltz's structural realism (more commonly known as neorealism) attaches a great deal of importance to the structure of the international system. In particular, neorealists focus on the structure of the international system rather than on human nature to account for the behavior of states.[12] They are also primarily concerned with the most powerful states, or great powers. Although this might seem shortsighted and insensitive, the explanation is quite simple. While war between two minor powers is tragic for those involved and affected by the war, it does not fundamentally change the international system. On the other hand, war between major powers has the ability to destroy the international system and, in modern times, could destroy human civilization. It is more important to focus on a potential war between the United States and Russia because their collective military power (nuclear, chemical, and advanced weapons) has the ability to radically alter the world and the people living in it. A war between Eritrea and Ethiopia, which did occur between 1998 and 2000 and killed tens of thousands of people, barely registered on the conscience of world politics because the effects were localized. Unfortunately, unlike a war between major powers, a war between lesser powers causes death, destruction, disease, and hardship within those countries, but the wider population does not feel the horrendous effects of the war and as a result, the implications are less of a concern.

To judge the potential politics about the system, the neorealists must first define the structure of the international system. The reason is that neorealists believe that the structure of the system is the primary cause of actor behavior. This is one of the major differentiating factors between classical realists and neorealists. The classical realists believe that human nature is the primary cause of state behavior while the neorealists believe the structure of the system is the cause. Thus, in order to understand neorealism, we must start with one simple question—what is structure? According to Waltz, structure is composed of three things: the ordering principles of the system, the characteristics of the units, and the distribution of capabilities amongst those units.

First, neorealism must define the ordering principles of the system. In other words, what is the primary organizational pattern of the system? This organizational pattern typically falls into one of two categories—hierarchy or anarchy. Building on the work of the classical realists, neorealists see the international system as a state of anarchy—meaning there is no accepted centralized political authority. This creates a system where states must engage in self-help if they are to provide for their own security. Simply put, no one else will do it for them. This differs from a hierarchical system, which contains a centralized authority that creates laws and enforces them. In a global community where there is no world police, army, or judges to turn to, states must behave in a fundamentally different way than if they lived in a hierarchical system. In an anarchical system, if a state is insecure, *it* must address the problem. For instance, if someone attacks you in a hierarchical system, there exists a means of recourse—you can call the police and allow them to rectify the situation. However, if attacked in an anarchical system, there is no one to call, no 911 to dial. You must deal with the situation and reestablish your own state of security. We will examine this idea of self-help at greater length later in this chapter.

Second, neorealists want to understand the character of the units. The units simply refer to the primary actors in the system and neorealists see states as the most important and indispensable actor in the international system. This means that spending time studying other actors, such as international organizations and nongovernmental organizations, is futile and pointless. States run the show, and their primary concern is their security, even to the point of obsession. The reason states exist is to provide security for land and people; thus, they have to be concerned with its continued presence. By considering a state as an actor, rather than individuals, neorealism also allows us to understand how states make decisions without delving into the minutia of each state's decision-making process. Ultimately, the process does not matter because in the end, states make decisions because they believe that decision will maximize their power. This does not mean there cannot be mistakes; humans are fallible and make mistakes all the time. There can be mistakes of misconception, bad information, and miscalculation. Yet, by not focusing on the process and instead focusing on outcomes, neorealist analyses allow for a parsimonious understanding or a very short description that explains a lot of world politics.

But beyond this obsession with security, what are the characteristics of these units or states? First, states are sovereign, meaning states are the source of final and absolute authority within their territory. Second, states are rational unitary actors.[13] This funny phrase essentially means that the apparatus of a state creates decisions that address the security concerns of the state. This apparatus works in concert with one another and speaks with one voice. The often-heard phrase is that when it comes to issues of foreign policy, politics stops at the water's edge. What this means is that the internal actors of a state will speak as one when it comes to issues of international security and that their decisions will be rational—or based on a Hobbesian-like cost/benefit analysis. Third, states have vulnerability. This simply means that states are always worried about their survival and, thus, always concerned with their security. Finally, states have negativity or a lack of trust. States do not trust other states and their ability to assist them in gaining security, thus perpetuating the self-help system described earlier.

The final characteristic of structure is the distribution of capabilities amongst these actors. According to neorealism, this is the one characteristic of structure that is prone to change. As Waltz stated, "The structure of the system changes with the changes in the distribution of capabilities across the system's units."[14] So, what are the capabilities Waltz is describing? Waltz, being a good realist, is analyzing the hard power (guns and money) that each state maintains and asking, what is the relative power each state holds? It is important to understand that relative power is power measured by comparing yourself to others. How much power does state A hold compared to, or relative to, state B? The distribution of capabilities is simply a comparison of relative power in the international system and an acknowledgment that where relative power resides can constantly change. At one point, state A may have a large amount of weaponry and economic power compared to others in the system, but that distribution of power can change, and as that distribution of power changes, the construct of the system changes.

In the end, by emphasizing structure what the neorealists are arguing is that there is limited agency of each individual. Individual decision makers have only a small impact on the direction of a state. It does not really matter who leads the states, because they can only make incremental changes. The focus on outcome, rather than process, troubles some observers of world politics.[15] For instance, when it comes to foreign affairs, there is little to no difference between a President Trump and a President Obama. According to neorealists, the difference is only incremental. The President of the United States, while powerful, is bounded by a governmental structure that limits their influence on decision making. Others in the United States make decisions and must carry out decisions, including Congress, the courts, the military, and a vast array of others. The two presidents might pursue different policies, but both are seeking to maximize the power of the United States and the security of their citizenry. Finally, regardless of who is president, it does not change the fact that the United States remains the most powerful country in the world. If you doubt this proposition, think about this: it is the office of President of the United States that makes these two men powerful, not vice versa. If you were to take either President Trump or President Obama and make them the leader of another country, say the Bahamas, you probably would never have heard of them no matter how great their political skills.

Distribution of Power as Prediction

Let us return to the distribution of power in the international system since that is the one area of change in the structure of the system. According to neorealists, the focus on the distribution of power among major states offers an opportunity for prediction, an area often lacking in IR theory. If you can tell a neorealist what the distribution of power in the international system is, then the neorealist can predict what the politics of the system will look like. Usually, we define the power structure of the international system in terms of polarity. Polarity refers to the arrangement or distribution of power in the international system.

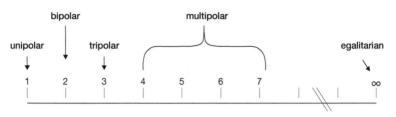

The number of major powers
in the system

Egalitarian system — where all powers have the same amount of power; this only
  occurs in theory.
Multipolar system — where four to seven powers are roughly equal in power.
  Scholars point to the time period between 1648 and 1914 in Europe as an
  example.
Tripolar system — where three powers have the majority of power. There are no
  good examples of tripolarity in the modern international system.
Bipolar system — where two powers are roughly equal and vie for power.
  Scholars point to the Cold War (1945-1991) between the United States and
  the Soviet Union as an example of a bipolar world.
Unipolar system — also known as a hegemonic system, where there is one
  preeminent power. An example would be Rome in the first century AD; some
  have argued that the United States after the Cold War might have experienced
  a unipolar system.

Figure 2.1   Potential Polarity Structures

Neorealists research to determine which kind of system is the most prone to conflict. Thus, the international system has different ways of classifying the distribution of power among states.

The three most observable forms that the modern international system has experienced are the multipolar system (Europe 1648–1914), the bipolar system (the Cold War between the United States and the Soviet Union 1945–1991), and the unipolar system (the United States after the Cold War). One of the great questions in structural realism is which of the three systems has provided the most stability (and peace). By examining the dynamics and evidence of each of the three systems, structural realists believe they can accurately describe the politics of these periods.

Multipolar

At one time, neorealist scholars saw the balance of power in the multipolar system as preferable, but now most think that either a bipolar or a unipolar system produces the most stability. The arguments as to why the bipolar or unipolar system is preferable are based upon the evidence from European politics of the nineteenth century and from logic games developed to try to explain the politics of the time. To begin an analysis of different power structures, let us consider some hypothetical ones first.

Imagine a world in which there are only two states: If state A is feeling insecure and increases its power, then state B must do the same or else have its security placed under threat. In a world that has three states, if state A increases its power, then state B can either increase its power or join in an alliance with state C to meet the security challenge presented by state A. In a five-state world, state B has three choices: to increase its power, to join in an alliance, or to do nothing and let states C, D, and E meet the security challenge of state A.[16] This *buck-passing* of responsibility, according to realists, can only occur in a multipolar system. A state might not be able to meet the rising cost of power accumulation and be forced to seek other methods. Nevertheless, buck-passing leads to a dangerous imbalance of power, which can only be corrected through war.[17]

In order to keep stability in a multipolar system, states have to engage in a balance of power, which can be expressed as the attempt to maintain a relative equality of power among the major states.[18] However, such a balancing game is very difficult to maintain and even harder to judge because there are so many machinations and eventualities. European states fought wars throughout the seventeenth and eighteenth centuries to maintain a balance between them. States fought wars, such as the War of the Spanish Succession (1701–1714), largely to prevent any one country from becoming too strong. The balance of power and alliance system has been widely held accountable for World War I. Though non-realists consider this system war-prone and even evil, policy makers considered it commonsense during the nineteenth century. One state does not necessarily want to impose its will or policies on other states, but it cannot allow other states to impose themselves on it. Therefore, it must be willing to engage in alliances to protect itself and must be willing to choose any partner as suitable. The difficulty is that when the alliances become hardened and rigid, states might decide that they must stick together, even when their interests might lie elsewhere.[19] The collapse of the multipolar system into World War I convinced most that balance of power politics was doomed and had devastating consequences.

This leaves neorealists with a debate about which kind of international system is the least prone to war. Some scholars believe that an international system that has two, roughly equal, powerful states (bipolar) is the best way to ensure stability and peace. They contend that peace is more likely when the two states are in rough parity. Each state is uncertain of victory in war, so they try to avoid it. Other scholars argue that the international system achieves stability when there is a system in which there is one major power (unipolar) that can establish rules and penalties. These scholars believe that peace is more likely to exist because the pecking order is quite unambiguous. The debate between these two schools is known as the *Parity versus Preponderance* debate, and it has generated contestation and research on both sides to support their claims.

Bipolar or Parity

One can picture a bipolar system as below, where the size of the blocks represents the power each state possesses.

Some scholars argue we are better off in a bipolar system because it is easier to balance power.[20] To make this argument scholars examine those time periods in which the world experienced a bipolar system and deduce how that system created or prevents stability. The most recent period is the Cold War (roughly 1945–1991). For many it seems counterintuitive that such a tense time in the world's history would be remembered as peaceful and stable; however, as the collapse of communist regimes in Eastern Europe was happening, John Mearsheimer wrote a famous piece entitled "Why We Will Soon Miss the Cold War."[21] Before reviewing his arguments, we should recall some of the dynamics of the Cold War.

The Cold War was an intense period in world politics where two major superpowers contested the dominance of the international

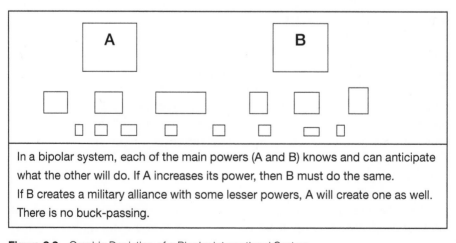

In a bipolar system, each of the main powers (A and B) knows and can anticipate what the other will do. If A increases its power, then B must do the same.
If B creates a military alliance with some lesser powers, A will create one as well. There is no buck-passing.

Figure 2.2 Graphic Depiction of a Bipolar International System

system: the United States and the Soviet Union. The two countries were allies during World War II (1939–1945), but it was an uneasy alliance, full of mistrust and misapprehension. After the war, the Soviet Union began creating a sphere of influence around its border. It occupied countries in Eastern Europe such as Poland, Romania, and Bulgaria. It actively sought friendly communist governments in countries such as Czechoslovakia, often through covert support of communist parties in those countries. Viewed from the perspective of the United States, the creation of a buffer zone around the Soviet Union through occupation and subversion was seen as a communist takeover, which threatened the United States and democracy worldwide.

The United States responded to the perceived Soviet threat with various policies, including the Truman Doctrine, NSC-68, the Marshall Plan, and the establishment of the North Atlantic Treaty Organization (NATO) in 1949. The Soviet Union responded with the creation of the Warsaw Pact in 1955. The most serious juncture of the Cold War was the Cuban Missile Crisis in October 1962 when the United States and the Soviet Union confronted each other over a showdown about the stationing of the Soviet nuclear missiles in Cuba. The crisis led the Kennedy Administration in the United States to believe that a nuclear exchange was not only possible but also likely. Although a nuclear exchange was averted during October 1962, there were a number of other close calls in which the Soviet Union and the United States almost exchanged nuclear weapons: during the Suez Crisis in 1974, the Berlin Crisis, and other instances of misunderstood moves. One author has calculated that there were sixteen significant nuclear crises during the Cold War.[22] There was a great deal of tension between the two countries over the course of the Cold War, and it makes people wonder why some realists might think that this international system would be preferable to others. Neorealists, like John Mearsheimer, point out that because there were only two powers, the calculations between the two countries were much easier. If one of the superpowers increased the number of weapons they had, the other had to do the same; if one side created a military alliance, then the other had to respond. There could be no buck-passing. Each side knew exactly what the calculations were and responded accordingly. Sure there were very tense situations, but because the calculations were easy to deduce, both sides could overcome the problems and deal with crises effectively. Thus, one scholar termed the period of tense relations between the United States and the Soviet Union "The Long Peace," and because both sides understood the implications and nuances of their relationship, they could avoid war.[23]

Most people think the Cold War was about ideology—that is, a democratic-capitalist system represented by the United States versus a Marxist-socialist system represented by the Soviet Union. Yet, the realists remind us that the focus of our inquiry about why the Cold War occurred should be about power. Both sides, but especially the Soviet Union, were insecure after World War II. The Soviet Union pursued policies that it thought would enhance its security (nuclear weapons, creation of buffer states).[24] The United States saw the same moves as inherently provocative. For realists, the focus on ideology is a blind alley; by focusing on power and the creation of the security dilemma, we are able to discern a more intellectual understanding of this time.

Unipolar or Preponderance

Critics of a bipolar system worry that this system is very dangerous.[25] In such a situation, hostilities can become long-term and dangerous. Because each side faces the same constant adversary, institutionalized paranoia (excessive irrational fear) will eventually set in. This institutional confrontation of a bipolar system leads some scholars to suggest that a unipolar (or hegemonic) system might be more stable.

The *hegemon*, as the preeminent power, can maintain peace and create stability in the international system. The so-called hegemon is usually the most powerful state in three realms—economic, political, military—and it is capable, willing, and legitimate in each realm. As

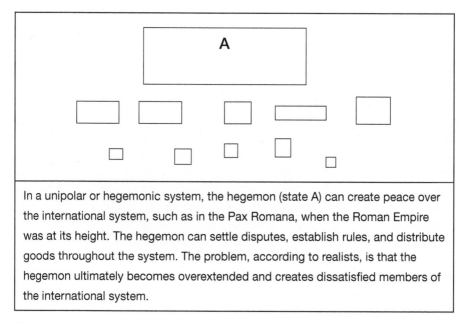

In a unipolar or hegemonic system, the hegemon (state A) can create peace over the international system, such as in the Pax Romana, when the Roman Empire was at its height. The hegemon can settle disputes, establish rules, and distribute goods throughout the system. The problem, according to realists, is that the hegemon ultimately becomes overextended and creates dissatisfied members of the international system.

Figure 2.3 Graphic Depiction of a Unipolar (Hegemonic) International System

the hegemonic power, it can use its power to distribute goods in the international system, establish the rules and rights in the system, and is the uppermost in the hierarchy of power in the system, whereas, in a bipolar system there is a lot of negotiation, in a unipolar system there is more deference.

The difficulty with a unipolar system, some neorealists argue, is that the system can only last for a very short time. One writer calls it a "unipolar moment" because other states will grow envious and tired of taking orders from a single state and work to undermine the system.[26] However, those scholars who are more inclined to see the stability of such a system will look toward the benefits of such a system. Once a state is preponderant, it sets the rules, encourages trade, and settles disputes. The currency of the country becomes the currency of trade in the world. The hegemonic power creates a general peace over the international system in which economies grow and societies flourish. Nevertheless, hegemons cannot afford to be hegemons forever; it has to spend its own resources (both treasure and blood) in order to maintain the international system.

While some have argued that there might be ways to forestall or delay the eventual decline,[27] realists generally agree that anarchy, insecurity, and the quest for power by all states will lead to the problems foreseen in both the bipolar and unipolar systems.

Putting It All Together: Using History to Explain Politics

One of the keys to understanding the realist perspective is to appreciate how realists understand history. Take, for example, Thucydides, one of the most famous of all Greek historians. Writing about four hundred years before the birth of Christ, Thucydides described the war between the Athenians and the Spartans. He opens the book by telling the reader that he will give an account of the arguments, jealousies, who did what to whom, who insulted the other, and so forth because he wants to demonstrate that all of this is superfluous. All of these issues were mere window dressing, interesting trivia that hid the real reason of war between Athens and Sparta. According to Thucydides, "The real reason for the war is, in my opinion, most likely to be disguised by such an argument. What made war inevitable was the growth of Athenian power and the fear which this caused in Sparta."[28] (Note: Thucydides is describing a security dilemma between the two rivals.)

Later in the manuscript, Thucydides discusses an encounter between Athens and the small city-state of Melos, known as the "Melian

Dialogue." The Melians were devoid of substantial power; they were a threat to neither Athens nor Sparta and were not even a significant source of additional power. Nevertheless, in 416 BCE, Melos refused to become a part of the Athenian alliance. The Athenians gave the Melians an ultimatum: Either you join our alliance, or we will destroy the city, kill all the men, and sell the women and children into slavery. First, the Melians argue that they want to be a friend to all, rather than an ally to one. But the Athenians dismiss this as a demonstration of their weakness rather than their strength. Then, the Melians appeal on the grounds of what is just; in effect, there would be no justice if the Athenians allowed the Melians to a choice. All appeals are for naught. The Melians refuse to submit to the alliance saying that they were unwilling to give up the freedom the city had enjoyed for seven hundred years. True to their word, the Athenians destroyed the city, killed all the men, and sold all the women and children into slavery. Thucydides summarizes the story by commenting that right and justice were only considerations between two sides that were relatively equal in power and that "the strong do what they can and the weak suffer what they must."[29] The phrase becomes an important encapsulation of how the realists understand the world. It is worth remembering the phrase because it is good shorthand to explain the realist perspective.

Realists look back at several events and writers in history and conclude that the utility of examining history and tracing power is particularly important. For example, Niccolò Machiavelli argued that a prince (a leader) should be merciful; however, his mercifulness should not interfere with his duty to afford protection to the state and its people. Thomas Hobbes similarly wrote that people willingly traded their freedom in exchange for security. This focus explains, according to realists, that issues such as morality, ideology, and religion play only a minor role in world politics. When push comes to shove, what matters is the insecurity of humans and the accumulation of power to address their insecurity. An important axiom for realists: People are always concerned with power and security, and you can empirically demonstrate this again and again.

History and the Security Dilemma

The realist perspective draws heavily upon historical analyses to explain politics, both past and present. The security dilemma has seemingly played an important role in driving world politics. Prior to World War I, several countries began building military capabilities because they thought that war was inevitable. In Germany, before the war, there was concern about the growing power of Russia. Russia was substantially increasing its army and building railroads toward the East. Germany concluded that if there was going to be a war, it was important to have it done and over with before Russia could finish building its strength. Germany had to build its military in order to protect itself.[30]

Great Britain viewed Germany's great military buildup with alarm. From the British perspective, there was no logical reason for Germany to construct a large fleet unless it planned to challenge the dominant position of the British Navy. Britain regarded its naval supremacy as absolutely necessary in order to protect the island nation from invasion and to guard its extensive overseas empire. Germany's policies thus heightened the security dilemma in Europe. By 1914, Germany was engaged in a naval arms race with Britain and, together with its ally Austria-Hungary, in a ground-force arms race with Russia and France. Realism points out the elegance of this story. Yes, Archduke Ferdinand was assassinated, and there was rising nationalism, competition, and so on. However, the realist maintains that these events and factors only lead us away from the main cause of World War I. The real reason for the war was the attempt by several countries to secure power in order to provide security, and the inevitable response by other countries as dictated by the security dilemma.

More recently, many scholars would point to the Cold War as evidence that the security dilemma plays an increasingly important role in world politics. World War II ended in 1945 when the United States dropped two atomic bombs on Japan. The wartime alliance between the United States and the Soviet Union was already demonstrating some significant strains as the war ended. Besides being a significant military resource, an atomic bomb was (and is) an expression of power and prestige; realists predict that because of the security dilemma other countries have no choice but to respond to this increase in relative power. Thus, by 1949, the Soviet Union had developed its own atomic weapon. It did so by engaging in a massive research project and through espionage (little did the United States know at the time that there was a spy at Los Alamos where the first testing took place in 1945).

From a realist perspective, the Soviet Union had no choice but to try to match, if not surpass, American technology and military might. The Soviet Union had to respond and develop its own weapon; if not, then it was vulnerable to an attack or subjugation from the United States. The Soviet Union used all means at its disposal to try to restore a balance of capabilities between the two. The United States, on the other hand, saw its use of nuclear weapons as no threat to anyone except Japan. It simply developed a weapon to help end the war. Yet, after the war, when the Soviet Union starting to work on its own nuclear program, the United States saw this need for the weapon as a challenge to its own position. The United States had its own worst fears confirmed: the Soviet Union was posing a challenge and threat to American security. As the Cold War continued, the American response to the Soviet military buildup was to increase its military spending and arms acquisition. The Soviets responded in a similar manner, which scholars have characterized as an arms race between the two countries.

This was true in other realms as well. In 1949, the United States and its allies created the NATO, which was a military alliance designed as protection from a potential attack from the Soviet Union. In 1955, the Soviet Union and its allies created a military alliance of its own, the Warsaw Pact, in response. In the late 1950s, the Soviet Union developed a space program and was the first to launch an artificial satellite and a manned spacecraft. This created apprehension and insecurity in the United States. The Americans worked feverously to do the same. Throughout the 1960s, both sides competed through their space programs, culminating in the 1969 moon landing by the United States. At first glance, this rivalry in space might appear to have little to do with security; however, it was clear that astronauts and cosmonauts were going to space on top of what were essentially large missiles. The space race was a demonstration of power. As the Cold War progressed, the two sides became increasingly wary of one another, and their insecurities mounted. Neither side could make an innocent move. Each move was seemingly calculated as a response to their own insecurity.

We can see other cases of the security dilemma in the world. India and Pakistan have had a long-running dispute that has occasionally boiled over into armed conflict since 1947. When the Pakistani prime minister Ali Bhutto was confronted with the prospect of India attaining nuclear weapons, he declared, "If India develops nuclear weapons, Pakistan will eat grass or leaves, even go hungry" in order to develop nuclear weapons as well. Some have claimed that Iran might want nuclear weapons to deter a potential attack from the United States or Israel, and North Korea has gone nuclear in an attempt to show their relative power. In all of these cases, one country feels insecure; however, their procurement of nuclear weapons would make others insecure as well.

Realists can explain more recent events as well. After the devastating attacks on New York and Washington, DC on September 11, 2001, the United States found itself increasingly insecure. After the initial military success in Afghanistan to deal with those who perpetrated the attacks, the United States began looking for other potential threats in the region. Iraq was a recalcitrant actor in world politics, and the United States accused its leader, Saddam Hussein, of supporting terrorist groups and actors. In the past, Saddam Hussein had sought nuclear weapons and used chemical weapons against Iran and on Shias in revolt. The United States launched the Iraq War as preventative (preemptive according to the Bush administration) against Iraq, because according to Condoleezza Rice, the United States could not wait for a smoking gun. If Iraq was seeking nuclear weapons, the United States had to deal with it sooner rather than later.

Notice that in each of the above accounts, the analysis stripped out concerns of ideology and morality. For the realist perspective (whether classical realist or neorealist), these factors are only likely to mask the real cause of conflict—the search for power in order to satisfy security needs. Thus, the factor that drives world politics is power. Nevertheless, we should also be cognizant of the fact that these power resources come with costs. Creating the resources that enhance a state's power requires finances. Thus, an economic policy that facilitates the maintenance of the security of the state is desirable.[31] It is a concept that is consistent whether in Thucydides' time or our own. And, as the security dilemma suggests, the pursuit of power often leaves others feeling less secure and creates a need for others to pursue power as well.

Wrap-Up

Here is the take-home message: This short overview has attempted to distill many different variations on realist thoughts into a few pages, and all of these variations are worth exploring and considering. But take notice of what the realists want you to do: not mix moral fervor with politics. Realists believe that statesmen were franker in the nineteenth century, at least among themselves, as to what they feared and what they wanted. They played for limited stakes. Utopians and idealists have sought to change world politics, but realists point out that the idea of trying to perfect government and people, creating permanent international peace, or the creation of empires that would last one thousand years did not appear until the nineteenth century. Realists argue that despite these attempts to change, humans remain the same. The same insecurities that drove politics 2500 years ago continue to motivate people today. Technology might have changed—humans have not.

Realism is an IR perspective that tries to distill a vast amount of information about world politics into a few digestible and easy prepositions. At its most basic, what drives all politics, especially world politics, is the pursuit of power. More broadly, realists focus on five core assumptions:

- The primary principle to study in world politics is power.
- The most important actors in world politics are sovereign states.
- Because the international system is in a state of anarchy, states must be obsessed with their own security.

- States seek to maximize their power so that they can provide for their own security. In fact, this is part of their human nature.
- In their quest for power and security, morality is not a driving factor.

Further Reading

1. John J. Mearsheimer, "Why We Will Soon Miss the Cold War" (1990a), provides a very readable account about why multipolarity might return to European politics following the end of the Cold War and the implications to the international system. His article in International Security (1990) builds upon the work and provides more nuance and academic justification to his argument.

2. E. H. Carr, *The Twenty Year Crisis, 1919–1939* (1946), provides a very important voice in the realist tradition. His work attempted to put the interwar period between World Wars I and II into perspective. Carr criticizes those (idealists) who believed that war and security issues could be overcome through political means. He also critiques those who believe that states can come to mutually shared interests through negotiations.

3. Daniel Mendelson's "Theatres of War: Why Battles over Ancient Athens Still Rage" (2004) account of why Thucydides and the Peloponnesian Wars still matter to world politics is a good account of how and why political scientists and IR theorists interpret history.

4. Hans Morgenthau, *Politics among Nations* (originally published in 1948), has gone through several editions, including several posthumously. The work remains one of the foundational pieces of modern realism, and Morgenthau touches on several topics and interpretations from a realist perspective. He also outlines and defines what political realism means in the modern world.

5. Kenneth Waltz, *Theory of International Politics* (1979), does much of the same thing for structural realism in his seminal work. Waltz, *Man, State and War: A Theoretical Analysis* (1959), also identifies why most of the motivations of state behavior occurs outside of the state in the international system.

6. John J. Mearsheimer, *The Tragedy of Great Power Politics* (2001), brings structural realism to the post–Cold War world in his analysis that demonstrates the logic of bipolar politics and employs a sizeable amount of information to make his case. Mearsheimer also helps to define a sub-school of thought known as "offensive realism," which posits that the need for security is not caused by human nature but on the nature of the international system.

Notes

1 Aside from these two primary forms of realism, other variants exist. These include offensive realism, defensive realism, and radical realism, among others. However, since this is an introduction to the theory, this chapter focuses on the two primary variants.

2 Hans J. Morgenthau. *Politics among Nations: The Struggle for Power and Peace*, Fifth Edition, Revised (New York: Alfred A. Knopf, 1973), 25.

3 Morgenthau, *Politics among Nations*, 4–12.

4 IR scholars usually refer to the current international system as the Westphalian system because its properties and primary rules were established under the Peace of Westphalia in 1648.

5 Thomas Hobbes, *Leviathan*. Edited with introduction by Edwin Curley (Indianapolis, IN: Hackett, 1651 [reprint 1994]).

6 Derek McKay and H. M. Scott. *The Rise of the Great Powers, 1648–1815* (London: Longman, 1983), 19–20.

7 This describes a Hobbesian state of nature, in which he states that life will be "solitary, poor, nasty, brutish and short."

8 Machiavelli provides the primary foundation for this principle, while Carr and Morgenthau bring it into contemporary international politics.

9 Morgenthau, *Politics among Nations*, 4.

10 John Spanier and Robert L. Wendzel, *Games Nations Play*, Ninth Edition (Washington, DC: CQ Press, 1996), 13; and Joel H. Rosenthal, *Righteous Realists* (Baton Rouge: Louisiana State University Press, 1991).

11 Robert O. Keohane. "Theory of World Politics: Structural Realism and Beyond," in *Political Science: The State of the Discipline*, ed. Ada W. Finifter (Washington, DC: American Political Science Association, 1983), 154.

12 Kenneth N. Waltz, *Theory of International Politics* (New York: Random House, 1979).

13 Stephen Krasner, "The Accomplishments of International Political Economy," in *International Theory: Positivism and Beyond*, ed. Steve Smith, Ken Booth, and Marysia Zalewski (Cambridge: Cambridge University Press, 1996).

14 Waltz, *Theory of International Politics*, 97.

15 This distinction has historically been a major point of difference between IR theorists and foreign policy scholars.

16 Perhaps like the United States during its isolation period.

17 See Thomas J. Christensen and Jack Snyder, "Chain Gangs and Passed Bucks: Predicting Alliance Patterns in Multipolarity." *International Organization* 44 no. 2 (1990): 137–38, for an overview of how realist thought understands buck-passing.

18 Kenneth N. Waltz, "International Structure, National Force, and the Balance of World Power." In *Theory and Reality in International Relations*, ed. John C. Farrell and Asa P. Smith (New York, London: Columbia University Press, 1967), 31–32.

19 F. S. Northedge, *The League of Nations: Its Life and Times, 1920–1946* (New York: Holmes and Meier, 1986), 22.

20 Waltz, *Theory of International Politics*; for others, who argue on the parity side, see Morgenthau and Mearsheimer.

21 John J. Mearsheimer, "Why We Will Soon Miss the Cold War," *The Atlantic Monthly* 266 no. 2 (1990a): 35–50.

[22] David Morgan, "Threats to Use Nuclear Weapons: The Sixteen Known Nuclear Crises of the Cold War, 1946–1985," *Ploughshares Monitor*, September 1, 1996.

[23] John Lewis Gaddis, *The Long Peace: Inquiries Into the History of the Cold War* (New York: Oxford University Press, 1987).

[24] X (George F. Kennan), "The Sources of Soviet Conduct," *Foreign Affairs* 25 no. 4 (1947): 566–82.

[25] Spanier and Wendzel, *Games Nations Play*.

[26] Charles Krauthammer, "The Unipolar Moment," *Foreign Affairs* 70 no. 1 (1990): 23–33.

[27] Some question this proposition. There is a debate about what might have been the effect if Nazi Germany was the hegemon instead of the United States. It is assumed that there would be no difference in the behavior of other states if the hegemon were destructive and abusive to other members of the system. Paul Kennedy (1987) suggests that there can be such a thing as a benign hegemony in which the leading state could farm out the costs of the maintenance of the international system and try to place in the structure a system that will exist (benefitting them) after the decline of the hegemon.

[28] Thucydides, *History of the Peloponnesian War*, trans. Rex Warner (New York: Penguin Books, 1972). Originally written 380 BCE, Book I, Chapter 1, paragraph 23, 49.

[29] Thucydides, *History of the Peloponnesian War*, Book 5, paragraph 89. The version that appears in Penguin Classics is translated as, "the strong so what they have the power to do and the weak accept what they have to accept" (402).

[30] Giles MacDonogh, *The Last Kaiser: The Life of Wilhelm II* (New York: St. Martin's Press, 2001), 352.

[31] That economic policy may take different forms, including mercantilism. See Michael P. Gerace, *Military Power, Conflict and Trade* (Portland, OR: Frank Cass, 2004); and David S. Landes, *The Unbound Prometheus: Technological Change and Industrial Development in Western Europe from 1750 to the Present* (London: Cambridge University Press, 1969).

Works Cited

Buzan, Barry, Charles Jones, and Richard Little. 1993. *The Logic of Anarchy: Neorealism to Structural Realism*. New York: Columbia University Press.

Carr, Edward Hallett. 1949. *The Twenty Years' Crisis 1919–1939: An Introduction to the Study of International Relations*. London: Macmillan.

Christensen, Thomas J., and Jack Snyder. 1990. "Chain Gangs and Passed Bucks: Predicting Alliance Patterns in Multipolarity." *International Organization*. 44, no. 2: 137–38.

Gaddis, John Lewis. 1986. "The Long Peace: Elements of Stability in the Postwar International System." *International Security*. 10, no. 4: 99–142.

Gaddis, John Lewis. 1987. *The Long Peace: Inquiries Into the History of the Cold War*. New York: Oxford University Press.

Gerace, Michael P. 2004. *Military Power, Conflict and Trade*. Portland, OR: Frank Cass.

Hobbes, Thomas. 1651 (reprint 1994). *Leviathan.* Edited with an introduction by Edwin Curley. Indianapolis, IN: Hackett.

Kennedy, Paul. 1987. *The Rise and Fall of Great Powers: Economic Change and Military Conflict from 1500 to 2000.* New York: Random House.

Keohane, Robert O. 1983. "Theory of World Politics: Structural Realism and Beyond." In Ada W. Finifter, ed. *Political Science: The State of the Discipline,* 503–40. Washington, DC: American Political Science Association. Reprinted in 1999. In Paul R. Viotti and Mark V. Kauppi, eds. *International Relations Theory: Realism, Pluralism, Globalism and Beyond.* Boston, MA: Allyn and Bacon.

Krasner, Stephen. 1996. "The Accomplishments of International Political Economy." In Steve Smith, Ken Booth, and Marysia Zalewski, eds. *International Theory: Positivism and Beyond.* Cambridge: Cambridge University Press, 102–11.

Krauthammer, Charles. 1990. "The Unipolar Moment." *Foreign Affairs.* 70, no. 1: 23–33.

Landes, David S. 1969. *The Unbound Prometheus: Technological Change and Industrial Development in Western Europe from 1750 to the Present.* London: Cambridge University Press.

MacDonogh, Giles. 2001. *The Last Kaiser: The Life of Wilhelm II.* New York: St. Martin's Press.

Machiavelli, Niccolo. 1532 (reprinted 1995). *The Prince,* edited with introduction by David Wootten. Indianapolis, IN: Hackett.

McKay, Derek, and H. M. Scott. 1983. *The Rise of the Great Powers, 1648–1815.* London: Longman.

Mearsheimer, John J. 1990. "Back to the Future: Instability in Europe after the Cold War." *International Security.* 15, no. 1: 5–56.

Mearsheimer, John J. 2001. *The Tragedy of Great Power Politics.* New York: W. W. Norton.

Mearsheimer, John J. 1990a. "Why We Will Soon Miss the Cold War." *The Atlantic Monthly.* 266, no. 2: 35–50.

Mendelsohn, Daniel. January 12, 2004. "Theatres of War: Why Battles over Ancient Athens Still Rage." *The New Yorker,* 79.

Morgan, David. September 1, 1996. "Threats to Use Nuclear Weapons: The Sixteen Known Nuclear Crises of the Cold War, 1946–1985." *Ploughshares Monitor.*

Morgenthau, Hans J. 1973. *Politics among Nations: The Struggle for Power and Peace,* Fifth Edition, Revised. New York: Alfred A. Knopf, 4–15.

Northedge, F. S. 1986. *The League of Nations: Its Life and Times, 1920–1946.* New York: Holmes and Meier.

Organski, A. F. K. 1968. *World Politics,* second edition. New York: Knopf.

Rosenthal, Joel H. 1991. *Righteous Realists.* Baton Rouge: Louisiana State University Press.

Sagan, Scott D. 2006. How to Keep the Bomb from Iran. *Foreign Affairs.* 85, no. 5: 45–59.

Spanier, John, and Robert L. Wendzel. 1996. *Games Nations Play,* Ninth Edition. Washington, DC: CQ Press.

Thucydides. 1972. *History of the Peloponnesian War.* Translated by Rex Warner. New York: Penguin Books. Originally written 380 BCE.

Waltz, Kenneth N. 1967. "International Structure, National Force, and the Balance of World Power." In John C. Farrell and Asa P. Smith, eds.

Theory and Reality in International Relations, 31–47. New York, London: Columbia University Press

Waltz, Kenneth N. 1959. *Man, State and War: A Theoretical Analysis.* New York: Columbia University Press.

Waltz, Kenneth N. 1979. *Theory of International Politics.* New York: Random House.

X (George F. Kennan). 1947. "The Sources of Soviet Conduct." *Foreign Affairs.* 25, no. 4: 566–82.

CHAPTER 3

Liberalism

Explaining the Presence of Cooperation

Eric K. Leonard

O f all the theories in international politics, liberalism may be the most disparate and fragmented. When I first began investigating IR theory as a graduate student, I found it interesting that a seemingly coherent theory could have so many variants. If one simply looks at many of the texts on IR theory, we see liberal variants ranging from classical liberalism, neoliberalism, and complex interdependence to pluralism, rationalist, rationalist democratic peace, and many others.[1] It becomes even more confusing if students start to examine this perspective from a foreign policy perspective as opposed to an international politics one or even layering in a domestic consideration of this term. However, if one looks closely at these liberal theories, there remain several core principles common to all.

The first of these is that cooperation amongst international actors is not only possible but that cooperation fulfills states' interests. Second, all liberals agree that war is not inevitable and that neither human nature nor the anarchic structure of the system dooms the system to a state of perpetual conflict and war. There is some disagreement amongst the liberals as to why war occurs, but they all believe its rectification is found in the formation of cooperative arrangements. In this regard, liberals remain less deterministic than their realist counterparts, who view conflict as an inevitable part of international politics. Third, liberals see the international system as an interdependent community in which not only the interests of all actors are intertwined but also the problems in the global system are transnational and therefore affect all. Fourth, liberals are less state-centric than their realist counterparts.

In other words, liberals generally believe that nonstate actors, such as intergovernmental organizations (IGOs), nongovernmental organizations (NGOs), multinational corporations (MNCs), and even individuals are influential and independent actors. However, it is important to recognize that neoliberalism backs off this principle a bit, but even this variant of liberalism still relaxes the realist state-centric assessment of global politics. Finally, liberals believe that progress and change are realistic goals for the global community. This change results from recognition of the preceding principles and the understanding that international actors can produce a more peaceful, cooperative system that fulfills their national interest. The spreading of democracy and the strengthening of free markets exemplify this change.[2] We will examine this prospect for change in greater detail at the conclusion of the chapter when discussing the formation of the International Criminal Court (ICC). Therefore, despite the disparate nature of liberals, the core remains intact throughout its theoretical evolution. The purpose of this chapter is to assist students in understanding that evolution and the distinction between liberalism and its main theoretical counterpart, realism.

Thinking Like a Liberal

Let us suppose that you have just received a review sheet for your first International Politics exam. Your primary interest in this situation is to pass, if not excel, in this exam. The question is how to achieve this interest. One way would be to study by yourself in the hope that you achieve a higher grade than your classmates do and gain a higher level of notoriety than your peers. However, this approach is predicated on a self-help method of achieving one's interests and thus creates a situation where assistance from others is not acceptable because others might cheat or free ride on your knowledge. They also might achieve a higher score, thus hurting your relative gains (both approaches being very realist in their approach and goal construction). But another means of achieving your interest is based on the notion that you and your peers share the common interest of passing the exam. And although you may have a certain level of expertise on the subject, your fellow classmates also have a high level of understanding that might be useful in passing (or even acing) the exam. As a result, you calculate that cooperating with your classmates may in fact result in a higher grade and the absolute achievement of your goal. Ultimately, the realization by students is that the act of cooperation can be beneficial to all parties without sacrificing self-interest. One just needs to view the world in terms of *absolute* gains, as opposed to the realist principle of *relative* gains (two terms that this chapter will clarify).

Foundational Principles

As stated earlier, liberal theory has a very disparate and oftentimes confusing lineage. As a result, this section of the chapter traces the evolution of liberal thought by discussing the foundational forms of liberalism, classical liberalism, and complex interdependence. It is important that students not lose sight of the core principles of liberalism discussed earlier because it is on these principles that all of the following perspectives build. After establishing this foundational piece of liberal theory, the chapter turns to a more detailed discussion of neoliberal thought. The reason for a more extensive discussion of this form of liberalism is that neoliberalism has gained the most prominence as a means of understanding the international system. Therefore, although students must understand the foundational ideas found in the classical forms of liberalism, the bulk of this chapter ultimately focuses on the neoliberal perspective and its "correction" of classical liberal thought.

Classical Liberalism or Interwar Liberalism

Classical liberalism or idealism (as the realists termed it) was part of the "first debate" in international relations theory in which they engaged the realist conception of the world as an anarchic place of perpetual conflict.[3] Contextually, this theory was a direct result of World War I, and its primary goal was to prevent such a horrific event from occurring again.[4] Such thinking built upon some of the greatest thinkers of political philosophy including Charles-Louis de Secondat Baron de La Brede et de Montesquieu and Immanuel Kant, both of whom provide theoretical answers to many of the realist understandings of why states go to war (as discussed in the previous chapter).

Montesquieu begins the foundational understanding of liberalism by focusing on the role that human nature plays in decision making. According to Montesquieu, human nature is not defective or prone to self-interested bouts of conflict. Conflict and war are the result of societal attributes and the competition amongst nations. Therefore, conflict and war are not an inherent part of humanity and by educating people, most notably those that might control the political apparatus that can initiate war and conflict, the global community can rectify these problems.[5]

Kant, on the other hand, emphasizes the mechanism by which states can overcome the anarchical nature of the international system. For Kant, the answer is very easy—states must engage in a form of collective security to protect their national interest and the interests of the global community. Such a federation of states would create an interdependent relationship amongst the world's actors, while not necessitating that they give up their sovereignty.[6] It is through these two foundational thinkers that classical liberals begin to construct an understanding of global politics. The result is four basic principles that provide the basis for classical liberal thought:

1. War and conflict are the result of irrational decision making.
2. These types of activities usually result from poor leadership and not mass public opinion.
3. Misunderstandings between leaders are the primary cause of war, not human nature or the anarchical structure.
4. The implementation of mediating structures (international organizations and international legal principles) can assist in rectifying these misunderstandings.[7]

Classical liberals generally believe that progress can occur and that the international community has the capability to alter the war-ravaged system of the early twentieth century into a more peaceful and stable system. As one scholar stated, "The distinctive characteristic of these writers [liberals] was their belief in progress: the belief, in particular, that the system of international relations that had given rise to World War I was capable of being transformed into a fundamentally more peaceful and just world order."[8]

In order to achieve such an idealistic goal, the classical liberal perspective advocates both the growth of international organizations and the election of a more enlightened leadership. In other words, if the international community is to prevent war, international actors (with an emphasis on state leadership and other domestic actors) must take action both at the international and domestic level. In attempting to prevent war, the first step is to establish a cooperative system in which discussion and mediation amongst nation-states take place within established organizational structures. These organizational structures serve as institutions within which states' conflicting views can be resolved peacefully. This line of thinking perceives the major cause of war as a lack of international organization (not just international organizations) and mediation. As Leonard Woolf explained, if we are to avoid war, then

> there must be international law and a regular method of making it; there must be organs of international government and organs for interpreting the law and settling disputes; there must be the machinery and procedure for common international actions and from making changes to meet changed conditions; there must be international control of national power and provision for common action in the face of a resort to war or the threat of war by any nation.[9]

According to classical liberals, the formation of international organizations and the promotion of international legal principles could very well serve as the mechanisms that prevent war. A major part of their role is the fact that these international organs of law and dispute settlement mechanisms assist in the prevention of misunderstandings between state leaders. In short, these institutions provide state leaders with a forum in which they could air their differences and possibly achieve a peaceful resolution. This is important because as stated earlier, interwar liberalism believes that misunderstandings amongst political leaders are one of the primary causes of war.

Along with the formation of these international organizations, liberal scholars also assert the need for better domestic leadership. The formation of mediating structures is not sufficient, and therefore, a group of enlightened leaders must complement these structures. In general, liberals view human nature in an optimistic manner. They see humanity as understanding right from wrong and having the capability to behave according to their internal moral compass. Along with this optimistic view of humanity, liberalism also perceives individuals as rational entities and war as an irrational act. As a result, an educated and enlightened individual can avoid the pursuit of war as a national policy because it is an illogical act. Therefore, one of the primary ways to prevent war is to instill leadership that understands right from wrong and uses this rational assessment as the basis for their decision making. With an enlightened leadership at the helm, the futility of war becomes self-evident and the initiation of war as a method of achieving one's foreign policy becomes unreasonable.

This initial description of classical liberal thought provides a clear demarcation between liberals and their classical realist counterparts. The first of these differences is the nonstate-centric manner in which liberals perceive the world. The classical liberals believe that individuals and international organizations play a profound role in the construct of the international system, thus providing a stark contrast with the more state-centric theory of realism. Second, the liberal perspective has a more optimistic view of human nature. Instead of viewing humanity as appetitive and desirous, liberals see human nature as good and just. They believe that humanity has the ability to act upon its internal moral compass or as one of my students put it, "their moral GPS" (as he explained to me, nobody carries a compass anymore). This provides classical liberals with the belief that change and cooperation can occur and the result is a more peaceful global community.

However, it is with this last claim that classical liberals falter in their understanding of international politics and where ultimately, the classical realists win out in the first debate. The problem, according to many critics, is not the claims of classical liberalism but the normative nature of such claims. If you recall from the introductory chapter, normative claims are those predicated on notions of what *should* the international system look like; while empirical claims are based on what *does* the international system look like. One of the most targeted criticisms of liberal thought is that this group of IR theorists makes claims of how the system should be constructed—cooperative and peaceful—without grounding such claims in an empirical conception of what the system actually looks like. Once World War II begins, IR theory relegates classical liberalism scholars to a secondary consideration for understanding world politics. Scholars deem the theory as factually inaccurate, which the introductory chapter makes clear is the single greatest failure of a theoretical perspective.

Despite this perceived shortcoming, the inception of liberalism as a theory of international relations provided scholars with the foundations for neoliberal institutionalism. Classical liberals noted the anarchical nature of the international system, the need for and the ability to achieve cooperation among states, and the positive role for international organizations. All of these attributes found their way into neoliberal thought, while others, like the importance of an educated leadership, were abandoned (or at least minimized) along the way. However, the evolutionary history of liberal thought has many more twists and turns, one of which is a need to impose a more empirical conception of the world into the theory. Let me now turn the readers' attention to the complex interdependence movement of the late 1970s and the more empirical arguments of an emerging cooperative world order.

Complex Interdependence

The second form of liberalism this chapter discusses is part of the 1970s' challenge to realist thought and is termed complex interdependence.[10] The main authors of this theory are Robert Keohane and Joseph Nye, who in their classic 1977 text establish the foundation for this novel theory.[11] Building on the previous liberal core, Keohane and Nye describe three main characteristics of a complex interdependence view of international relations: (a) multiple channels of interaction, (b) an absence of hierarchy amongst the world's issues, and (c) due to the presence of complex interdependence, the realist focus on military force for achieving one's interests is no longer a given.

Beginning with the first proposition, complex interdependence asserts that multiple channels of contact have the effect of connecting the world's different societies. According to this perspective, a web of interaction exists amongst the community of international actors, thus creating an atmosphere of interdependence. This interdependence occurs through interstate, transgovernmental, and transnational relations, all of which bind the global community's governmental and nongovernmental entities together.

Let us begin with the notion of interstate interaction. This form of interaction is state to state—a very realist conception of international politics, as readers saw in the previous chapter. This is important because a common misconception of complex interdependence theory is that it believes the state is withering away. However, this perspective never argues that state-to-state interaction is irrelevant. Therefore, this theory is not about a "loss of the state" in global politics; instead, it is about a set of complementary understandings of actors and how they interact.

These complementary forms of interaction begin with the notion of transgovernmental relations. Transgovernmental relations are those interactions that occur between government actors that exist within states. Such actors typically include government officials such as presidents, prime ministers, diplomats, and others. In essence, this form of interaction calls into question the realist perspective that states are unitary actors. According to the complex interdependence theory, states are not unitary, and there are competing voices within the state that interact with other competing voices in other states.

Complex interdependence also views transnational relations as influential. These interactions are ones that occur between nonstate actors—such as MNCs, NGOs, IGOs, and others. This perspective builds on the foundational principles of classical liberalism and relaxes the state-centric notion of realism (as did the previous importance on domestic state actors) and places a significant emphasis on actors such as the United Nations, World Trade Organization, Amnesty International, and countless others. Of course, these relations also occur between nonstate actors, states, and government officials. The result is a more complex conceptualization of international politics in which a multiplicity of actors can exert influence.

Simply put, complex interdependence theory believes that the connections between global actors need not be solely intergovernmental. A multiplicity of channels exist, all of which perpetuate greater cooperation among these diverse actors and initiate a cooperative means of dealing with the world's transnational problems. Keohane and Nye cite major international airports as one example that "confirm(s) the existence of multiple channels of contact among advanced industrial countries."[12]

What is important about this proposition is that Keohane and Nye assert that the number of ways that societies interact has greatly expanded. It is no longer simply state elites meeting within the bounds of foreign offices. According to this theory, the multiple channels that tie societies together now consist of formal and informal interaction amongst both government elites and nongovernment elites (such as MNCs, international banks, etc.).

Complex interdependence also asserts that the number of issues affecting the world's international actors has become much larger and more diverse. Due to this expansion of international issues, Keohane and Nye argue that the primary determinant of foreign policy is not always going to be military security issues. Other issues, such as economic, social, and domestic issues all play a role in foreign policy formulation and as a result, there is no hierarchy of issues. This proposition is radically different from the mainstream thinking of that time, as discussed in the previous chapter on realism, which stipulates that military and security issues always assume primacy over other issues. Complex interdependence alters that perception and argues that military and security issues do not and should not dominate the foreign policy agenda of the world's nation-states. The result is a web of multiple, overlapping issues that all demand attention. Because there is such a plethora of issues facing international actors, Keohane and Nye believe that the necessity of international organizations, for functional reasons, is compelling. According to their theory, the global community only finds viable management or solutions to the world's interdependent issues through the establishment and use of international organizations.

Finally, reverting to the original goal of interwar liberals, complex interdependence theorizes that with an increase in state interdependence, the likelihood of war diminishes—at least among highly industrialized states. This does not mean that the use of military force is obsolete. What Keohane and Nye propose is that by tying two governments together in an interdependent relationship, the use of force between these two states is no longer the primary policy option. This is due to the cost, relatively calculated by the states, and uncertainty of war. However, the inception of more and more international organizations also alleviates the prospect of war by increasing interdependence. Thus, the result of this increased interdependence is, at least to some extent, the achievement of the interwar liberal's goal—mitigating conflict. The difference resides in the fact that complex interdependence theorists can understand this outcome via empirical conceptualizations as opposed to the more normative understandings that inspired the classical liberal approach.

Power also plays a role in interdependence theory and in order to understand this role, Keohane and Nye introduce two measurements of power within interdependent relationships: sensitivity and vulnerability. Sensitivity refers to the degree of "responsiveness within a policy framework." In other words, sensitivity refers to an actor's perceived effect of policy change within an interdependent relationship. If one country is sensitive to an alteration in the interdependent relationship, then that country is clearly at a power disadvantage.

However, sensitivity is not the only dimension of power within an interdependent relationship; one must also account for vulnerability. Vulnerability "rests on the relative availability and costliness of the alternatives that various actors face."[13] In other words, if the original relationship breaks down, the costs incurred by actors in implementing alternative policies would be a measure of vulnerability. Keohane and Nye use the following example: "Two countries, each importing 35 percent of their petroleum needs, may seem equally sensitive to a rise in prices; but if one could shift to domestic sources at moderate costs, and the other had no such alternative, the second state would be more vulnerable than the first."[14]

Thus, in analyzing global relations within the complex interdependence paradigm, one must account for the dyadic power dimensions of sensitivity and vulnerability. According to complex interdependence theorists, by grounding one's analysis of power within this dyadic or binary model, international relations scholars should be better able to predict bargaining advantages and, to some extent, outcomes.

Complex interdependence is the definitive liberal precursor to neoliberal institutionalism. Through the historical evolution of this theoretical perspective, scholars have altered certain attributes of liberalism, while discarding others. However, the core of the liberal tradition remains—international relations is not simply about power and coercion; it is often about cooperation, cooperation for the purpose of achieving common interests and alleviating the cost of unilateral action.

Neoliberal Institutionalism

The final form of liberalism this chapter will discuss is termed neoliberal institutionalism (NLI) or simply neoliberalism. NLI maintains the core of liberal thought but also strays from many of the principles of their theoretical predecessors. This is best exemplified by the fact that its primary author is also one of the primary authors of complex interdependence, Robert Keohane. One of the first things that students will recognize is that NLI is not as wedded to the classical liberal tradition as complex interdependence. This shows the evolution of Keohane's thinking on cooperation and its place within global politics. Students must also recognize that although NLI attempts to rectify the problems of previous liberal thinkers, it also attempts to resolve those found in neorealist thought. As Robert Keohane stated in 1993,

> [I]t is crucial to remember that it [neoliberal institutionalism] borrows as much from realism as from liberalism: it cannot be encapsulated as simply a "liberal" theory opposed at all points to realism. Indeed, it is almost as misleading to refer to it as liberal as to give it the tag of neorealism.[15]

In order to simplify this form of liberalism, this chapter breaks it down to six basic principles:[16]

1. States are the primary units of analysis.
2. States are rational unitary actors.
3. States exist within an anarchical system.
4. Complementary interests exist among states, therefore, cooperation is possible.
5. Relative gains are conditional.
6. Hegemony is not a necessary factor for cooperation.

As stated above, this preliminary list of neoliberal attributes clearly shows the debt Keohane owes not only to previous liberal thinkers but also to neorealism. Neoliberalism does deal with the act of cooperation among actors and the interest-based rationale for this type of action, but it also deals with concepts like anarchy, self-interest, and nation-states. These latter concepts are directly attributable to realist/neorealist thinking and its fundamental principles. Nevertheless, one should not assume that neoliberalism is simply a derivative of Ken Waltz and neorealism. There are fundamental differences between these two schools of thought, most notably in the outcomes perceived by neoliberal thinking. We will return to these differences at the conclusion of our discussion, just as a means of reiterating and emphasizing certain variations. But for now, let us begin with a discussion of those six core principles that create a coherent neoliberal perspective.

State-Centered

Breaking from most of his liberal predecessors and aligning himself with a core realist understanding, Robert Keohane asserts a much more state-centered theory than past liberal iterations. Many of Keohane's liberal ancestors viewed the state as the primary obstacle to cooperation and peace, and yet, neoliberal thinking emphasizes the primacy of the state.

Obviously, international institutions are important to the neoliberal rationale, but Keohane reminds us that these institutions are constructed of and by states and these states are pursuing their self (national)-interest.

Keohane does note that if we were to relax this premise (the state-centered nature of the system), cooperation could still occur. In other words, if states were not the major influential political entities in the world, Keohane still believes that cooperation would occur between transnational entities and regimes.[17] It is a common misconception that this addendum to Keohane's theory is an invitation for neoliberals to not only analyze but also emphasize the influence of nonstate actors. I wish to correct that misconception by stating that at no time within his writings does Keohane relinquish the premise that states are the primary actors in world politics. He acknowledges the importance of transnational actors, but never considers them the central unit of analysis. Therefore, rather than perceiving this statement as an invitation for neoliberal scholars to study nonstate actors, scholars should view it as a reassertion that, at this point in time, states are still the major unit of analysis for international relations and neoliberalism. His assertion that relaxing the state-centric paradigm does not hinder cooperation is simply a hypothetical situation that allows the reader to see that cooperation under anarchy is not contingent on states being the key actors. To reiterate, this does not mean that neoliberals view transnational actors as the primary units of analysis. As Keohane reasserts in 1995, "institutionalist theory [neoliberalism] assumes that states are the principal actors in world politics."[18]

Rational Unitary Actors

The second principle of NLI is that states are rational-unitary actors that seek to fulfill their self or national interests. Neoliberalism expects states to behave as rational egoists. In other words, their motivation for action is the pursuit of their own self-interest. This assumption is indistinguishable from the core premises of realist theory, except that the outcome of this rational egoism is not a Hobbesian state of nature in which everyone is at war with everyone.[19] Instead, this premise leads neoliberals to believe that cooperation and institution building is the rational behavior of nation-states seeking to fulfill their self-interest.

The distinction in the neorealist and neoliberal positions turns on the premise that when states pursue their self-interest, this does not preclude a mutuality of interests. According to the neoliberals, in many instances, states do share common interests, and this makes cooperation plausible. This is a key component of NLI because, without a mutuality of interests, cooperation is virtually impossible. However, it is equally important to note that a mutuality of interests between states does not automatically result in cooperative arrangements. Harmony is different from cooperation. Therefore, according to NLI, despite the mutuality of interests, there are times when cooperation fails. I will return to this point when discussing why cooperation within an anarchical system is possible.

Anarchy

The next premise of NLI is that states exist in an anarchical system. Again, things are looking quite realist. Robert Keohane and another neoliberal thinker, Robert Axelrod, define anarchy as "a lack of common government in world politics, not . . . a denial that an international society . . . exists."[20] NLI perceives this state of anarchy as a constant, but this does not mean that structured interaction does not exist amongst the world's states. Thus, neoliberals accept anarchy, or a lack of centralized government, as an attribute of world politics—making them look quite realist; however, unlike realism, neoliberals do not believe that this characteristic severely hampers or prevents cooperation from occurring. Common interests exist between states, and as a result, cooperation occurs.

Nevertheless, this cooperation exists within an anarchical system, and NLI acknowledges the fact that the structure of the system has a large impact on states' behavior. As a result, neoliberalism asserts a strong, yet not exclusionary, systemic approach to international relations. The anarchical system impacts state actions, but unlike the neorealist logic that theorizes that this type of system leads to a war of all against all, neoliberals see cooperation occurring within the anarchical system.[21] A return to the previous discussion of complementary interests explains why.

Common Interests

As I already stated, neoliberals assert that common or complementary interests exist among states. They cite these complementary interests as necessary conditions for cooperation, but not sufficient in and of themselves for cooperation. So how and why does cooperation occur within an anarchical system?

Keohane and other neoliberals accept a mutuality of interests among states as an empirical reality but contend that this still does not result in automatic cooperation among these actors. The primary reason is that cooperation is not synonymous with harmony. If states resided in a system of absolute common interest (harmony), then cooperation would not be necessary. The existence of a harmony of interests among states simply allows these states to pursue their self-interest with the knowledge that all other actors in the system hold complementary interests. As Keohane states, "Harmony refers to a situation in which actors' policies . . . automatically facilitate the attainment of others' goals."[22] The result is an apolitical system in which regimes and IGOs are unnecessary because cooperation already exists. If everyone holds the same interests, then cooperation is a given because the community of states is already pursuing the same harmonious goal.

Nevertheless, the international system is not a harmonious one. Instead, it is fraught with conflict and the inception of cooperation is simply a reaction to that conflict. In other words, if the system were void of any discord, the creation of cooperative arrangements becomes unnecessary. But because the system is not a harmonious one, cooperation becomes a mechanism or a means by which states achieve their common goals regardless of the anarchy that exists around them. According to Keohane, "intergovernmental cooperation takes place when the policies actually followed by one government are regarded by its partners as facilitating realization of their own objectives, as the result of a process of policy coordination."[23]

This distinction between harmony and cooperation helps us to define cooperation, but it does not tell us why states cooperate. Keohane shows us that harmony is not a central part of the world system and that cooperation is a possible solution to the discord that exists. If states choose to cooperate, one could view this action as an attempt to initiate an environment in which states can fulfill their mutual interests. But what are the reasons for state cooperation?

In order to address this question, it is necessary to combine all that we now understand about NLI and apply it to the anarchical international system. According to NLI, cooperation occurs because states act primarily as rational egoists who share mutual interests. The most efficient way to achieve utility maximization (simply put, fulfilling their interests) is through the formation of a regime or international institution. Regimes, as defined in an earlier footnote, are "sets of implicit or explicit principles, norms rules or decision-making procedures around which actors' expectations converge in a given issue-area." So regimes act as facilitators of cooperation by providing states with information, reducing uncertainty among states, reducing transaction costs, and establishing expectations concerning actors' behavior. In other words, regimes make cooperation a more palatable and efficient option. By lowering costs and providing information, regimes act to facilitate cooperation by limiting uncertainty and showing states the mutual benefits of cooperation. Therefore, despite the self-interested egoism of states, cooperation is possible because the mutuality of interests is, or can become, common knowledge among states.

The actualization of these interests occurs through the formation of regimes. States form regimes as a method of gaining their exogenously given goals. Put more simply, states believe that the benefits derived from cooperation far outweigh those of unilateral action. Therefore, states acting in a rational manner naturally form regimes to increase their personal gains. One can view this formation process as part of a strategic game, undertaken by states, in which they wish to further their interests through cooperation. Through institution building, states are able to gain their exogenously given interests. It is important to emphasize that state's interests are *a priori* (or exist prior to) regime formation; regimes do not define state's interest (this will be a significant difference between neoliberalism and social constructivism). Therefore, cooperation is simply a method by which a state obtains their previously defined, exogenously given interests.

It is now apparent that the premise of exogenously given interests is crucial to an understanding of NLI. This premise is deeply rooted in the realist aspect of this theory and assumes that states maintain a set of *a priori* interests. As a result, NLI does not consider state's interests as dynamic but institutional preference is. According to Keohane,

> I neither explore how economic conditions affect patterns of interests, nor do I investigate the effects of ideas and ideals on state behavior. The theory that I [Keohane] develop takes the existence of mutual interests as given and examines the conditions under which they will lead to cooperation.[24]

As the global environment changes, so too will the institutional preference for achieving states' *a priori* interests. Thus, it is at the point where these exogenously given interests overlap with other actors' interests that cooperation is a possibility.[25]

Relative versus Absolute Gains

This brings us to the next premise of NLI—states are not solely concerned with relative gains, as the realists would have us believe. Relative gains are simply gains that a state calculates by considering how much they gain in comparison, or relative to, other states. If states were only concerned with relative gains, this would seriously limit the prospects for cooperation. However, empirical reality shows us that cooperation exists in all areas of international politics. In other words, we see cooperation all around us. This is not to say, as many neorealists assert, that relative gains are a non-factor for neoliberalists. Keohane acknowledges the importance of relative gains to nation-states, but views these gains as highly conditional. Relative gains are only important when a state's *intent* upon receiving those gains is to use them against another state. Therefore, it is important to evaluate not only the capabilities of a state (as the realists do) but also its intentions (which is what the neoliberals do). If a state accrues asymmetrical gains from a cooperative relationship (they gain a whole lot more than someone else), but their intent is not to dominate another state, then the relative gains are insignificant. In other words, if you trust the other party, the fact that you do not gain as much as him/her is irrelevant and cooperation will occur. In such a situation, it is the absolute gains (the fact that the actor gains something) that matter most. In essence, whether or not a state achieves greater relative gains through cooperation is not foremost in the participants' mind; it is the absolute gains accrued by each actor that matters most or the fact that you gain something from the cooperative arrangement. If the intention of a state to dominate other states were abundantly clear, then neoliberals would concede the fact that a consideration of relative gains is now a fundamental part of the foreign policy evaluation. And subsequently, if relative gains were part of the decision-making process, then neoliberals would have to admit that the prospect for cooperation between states is minimal.

Keohane goes on to show that in cooperative situations involving multiple actors, the concept of relative gains becomes even more insignificant. In such a situation, the question becomes which relationship prevents cooperation? If state A gains relative to state B, but not to state C or D, will state A cooperate? A neoliberal perspective concludes that scholars cannot adequately address this situation unless they know the *intentions* of each state, not just their capabilities. If state C or D does not intend to use their relative gains against state A because they are allies, then state A cooperates because of their ability to accrue absolute gains. In such a situation, neoliberal institutionalists would not consider relative gains a detrimental factor to cooperation. However, if state C does intend to use their gains against state A, then state A does not cooperate despite the possibility of absolute gains. The point Keohane is trying to make is that relative gains are conditional and, therefore, they will not always act as an obstacle to cooperation. If relative gains are not part of the evaluation, because intent to harm and absolute gains exist, then cooperation under anarchy is not only possible, but also probable.

Hegemony

The final premise of NLI concerns the concept hegemony. IR scholars define hegemony as the dominance and leadership of one state in the international system, thus projecting power over all other states.[26] Neorealist and power-based theories assert that hegemony is a necessary component for regime formation and cooperation. According to their thinking on world politics, a hegemon, because they are so powerful relative to other states, can coerce states to cooperate. This form of cooperation is more about imposed interests than mutual interests. NLI counters this coercive cooperation argument by stating that regime formation and maintenance can occur without a nation-state acting as a hegemon. Throughout his 1984 text, Keohane constantly refers to post-hegemonic cooperation. At one point in the text, Keohane states that

> without ignoring the difficulties that beset attempts to coordinate policy in the absence of hegemony, this book contends that non-hegemonic cooperation is possible, and that it can be facilitated by international regimes . . . Cooperation is possible after hegemony not only because shared interests can lead to the creation of regimes, but also because the conditions for maintaining existing international regimes are less demanding than those required for creating them.[27]

Clearly, the neoliberal thought does not necessitate the existence of a hegemon for cooperation to occur; as this chapter has already shown, neoliberals see cooperation occurring as the result of shared interests among states and the ascertaining of absolute gains through regime formation. Although hegemony may assist in the formation process, neoliberalism does not believe that hegemonic coercion plays a primary role in this process. As a result, neoliberals view power-based theories of cooperation as a misconception of the current global system.

Neoliberalism and Neorealism

So, in the end, what are the main points of disagreement between the neorealists and neoliberals? The understanding that realist thought is a power-based theory while neoliberalism is interest-based best sums up the primary difference between these two schools of thought. Both perspectives agree that the system is anarchical and states are attempting to maximize their self-interest. However, the result of this anarchy is vastly different. For neorealists, the result is a system of perpetual conflict with little to no cooperation. Any cooperation that does occur is the result of hegemonic coercion and control over the system. For NLI, anarchy exists, but it does not naturally result in a constant state of conflict. In fact, because states recognize that they have mutual interests, there can be a substantial amount of cooperation. Neoliberals acknowledge that hegemony can be helpful in the formation process, but it is not the dominant causal factor for actor behavior. As a result, if the hegemon's power declines, the cooperative arrangement or regime that the international community created persists. This is due to the fact that members of the international community, or at least those participating in the regime, have invested a large amount in the formation process of the regime, have gained from this regime, and do not want to lose their investment. Therefore, when analyzing the formation of any IGO from an institutionalist perspective, the primary reason for its formation must be complementary or overlapping interests. It is this causal factor for behavior that allows for cooperation and the ability to overcome the Hobbesian state of war that realists believe is inevitable.

Putting It All Together: Cooperation to End Impunity

As students should now recognize, despite the differences in the distinctive forms of liberalism, they all complement one another and the alterations from theoretical form to theoretical form result from a need for the theory to evolve and grow both intellectually and in terms of the changing international context. So if one is to apply liberalism, in its broadest interpretation, as a way to explain, understand, and possibly predict the current and future events of global politics, what does this look like? This differs depending on the issue area being discussed (economics, war/conflict, human rights, etc.), but at this point, I will look at one of their most prolific applications, international institution building, specifically within the realm of human rights.

It is important that students understand that I do not intend this section to be an extensive case study on the ICC formation process or a definitive empirical justification for the benefits of liberalism. The intent of this discussion is to provide students with a broad description of the events leading up to the formation of the ICC and how the liberal perspective might understand this process. As a result, students should consider the primary principles of liberalism (cooperation assists in fulfilling interests, war is not inevitable, interdependence is an empirical fact, nonstate actors are influential, and progress is possible) when reading this section in an attempt to assess its theoretical viability.

Forming the ICC

During the summer of 1998, the global community of nation-states and human rights NGOs descended on Rome to discuss the possible formation of a permanent ICC. During the Rome Conference it became evident that a large number of state and nonstate actors approved of the formation of an ICC. This overwhelming support for the Rome

Statute (as the final treaty forming the ICC was entitled) exemplifies the neoliberal idea that cooperation among states is possible despite the anarchical nature of the world system. This support was solidified on April 11, 2002, when the requisite number of ratifications occurred, thus bringing the Rome Statute into force on July 1, 2002. The final outcome of the Rome Conference was an overwhelming support of the Statute, despite the presence of at least two competing positions concerning the construction of the ICC. So as scholars of international politics, how do we understand this process, and does this understanding provide us any insight, possibly predictive capabilities, about future international organization formation processes?

Pursuing these questions from a liberal or neoliberal perspective leads us to the negotiating process among states and other influential actors. The foundation of cooperation within this issue lies with the Draft Statute for an ICC published by the International Law Commission in 1994. State delegates employed this document during the pre-Rome negotiations (PrepCom) in an attempt to create a draft statute for a permanent ICC. This was by no means an easy task. Over a three-year period, the PrepCom participants struggled to form a final draft Statute that would serve as an acceptable foundation for a diplomatic conference. Over six PrepCom sessions and numerous informal sessions delegates amended, altered, and transformed the 1994 Draft Statute until the working text contained 116 articles, with several options and hundreds of brackets.

During this three-year process, the positioning of the participant states began to take shape. The first group, the Like-Minded Group, was composed of mostly western European states that desired an independent and far-reaching court. Although the Like-Minded Group formed around the time of the ILC Draft Statute, it was not until December 1997 that they stated their foundational principles. The principles included an independent prosecutor and a court with universal jurisdiction. At this point, the P-5, which originally included the permanent five members of the Security Council (the United States, China, France, Russia, and the United Kingdom) but slowly dwindled to the United States, China, and other non-P-5 states, had also established their position on the Statute. These states wanted a court that could only initiate proceedings with Security Council consent and would embody a strict understanding/interpretation of state sovereignty.

With these two competing and seemingly opposing positions carved out before the Rome Conference, it became obvious to both sides that without high-level cooperation the formation of a permanent ICC would be impossible. Thus, during both the PrepCom meetings and the Rome

Conference, it became evident to both groups of states that they would have to make concessions. Notice that the interest to end impunity and bring to justice those that commit the most heinous crimes existed first. The formation of the regime took shape because of this shared interest.

However, at least one other actor played a fundamental and influential role in this process—a coalition of human rights NGOs known as the Coalition for the International Criminal Court (CICC). This group of NGOs came together to support a similar agenda as the Like-Minded Group and provided what many observers of the negotiation process believe was the final impetus to the approval of the Rome Statute. This group of nonstate actors assisted in educating delegates, providing information to the public via newsletters and their webpage, and facilitating meetings amongst the competing factions, among other things. Their role as a source of knowledge and expertise on this issue cannot be ignored and simply shows their influence on the proceedings.

Many observers of the formation process see the ICC's approval as a loss for the United States and a win for human rights advocates, in particular the NGO community, and western European nation-states. One way to assess whether this is true is to analyze the gains and losses of the United States delegation. If this is a truly realist process, the involved parties will not give on anything that hurts their relative power. However, if the liberals are correct, the United States (and others) will grant concessions if the intent of the member states is not to harm U.S. interests. Remember, the United States is not opposed to a method of ending impunity; that is a shared interest that the United States has with the rest of the world. The United States is more concerned with how the international community intends to implement this shared interest.

At the close of the Rome Conference, the United States felt that the Statute needed a tremendous amount of alteration. This opposition to the Rome Statute is why the United States never moved toward ratification. Nevertheless, this does not mean that the United States and the rest of the opposition states did not make significant gains during the negotiation process. According to the main U.S. diplomat to the negotiation process, David Scheffer, the P-5 states achieved numerous objectives prior to and during discussions at Rome. Ironically, the successful implementation of some of the P-5's objectives may have resulted in the ultimate defection of the United Kingdom, France, and Russia from the P-5 group.

First, the United States felt that they had gained an improved form of complementarity in terms of jurisdiction of the Court and its ability to pursue prosecution. Under the principle of complementarity, the ICC must defer to a state's national courts. Only if the national court is unable or unwilling to prosecute the case does the ICC have jurisdiction.[28] This principle protects the national sovereignty of state parties and upholds the premise of *ne bis in idem* (double jeopardy). As a result, although the United States did not achieve the exact form of jurisdictional control they desired (Security Council control), Scheffer did admit that it was an improvement over the previous form and was clearly a concession by the Like-Minded/CICC group.

Second, the final Statute granted the UN Security Council the power to halt the Court's action in certain circumstances. According to Article 16 of the Rome Statute,

> No investigation or prosecution may be commenced or proceeded with under this Statute for a period of 12 months after the Security Council, in a resolution adopted under Chapter VII of the Charter of the United Nations, has requested the Court to that effect; that request may be renewed by the Council under the same conditions.

Thus, the role of Article 16 is to provide the Security Council with a mechanism through which they can stop or prevent an ICC investigation or prosecution. This component was crucial to the United States because it provides them with greater authority over the initiation of investigations and the possible prosecution of individuals by the ICC; both issues that the United States deeply desired.

Third, the Rome Statute upholds the confidentiality of national security information. Article 72 of the Rome Statute declares that in instances where a state believes that the disclosure of information or documents will prejudice the national security of that state, they have the right to "intervene in order to obtain resolution of the issue." In short, the Article provides states with the ability to block the introduction of certain testimony or evidence into the Court proceedings if that state deems it a threat to their national security. This Article is another way in which the ICC upholds the norm of state sovereignty, an ideal that the United States holds in high regard.

Fourth, major parts of the Rome Statute included principles of due process and the protection of the accused. The Rome Statute's Articles 55, 66, and 67 deal with the rights of the accused and clearly parallel American domestic judicial proceedings. These articles provide the accused with the right to be promptly informed of their alleged crimes, the right to remain silent, the presumption of innocence, the right to have adequate time and facilities to prepare for a defense, the right to counsel, the right to a timely trial, the right to the assistance of a competent interpreter, and others. Clearly, the participants of the Rome

Conference wanted to uphold the individual rights that the United States holds so dear, and this desire is embodied, much to Scheffer's delight, in the final Statute.

Fifth, the Statute established rigorous qualifications for the appointment of judges. As per Article 36.3-8, nominated individuals shall be of a high moral character and exhibit competence in the proceedings of not only criminal law and procedure but also international humanitarian law and the law of human rights. The election process entails a secret ballot vote by the Assembly of State parties and the result of that election is that no two judges shall be from the same state. The United States saw the need for rigorous qualifications and election proceedings because this would provide the Court with the ability to fight against any form of politicization that might impinge on its ultimate goal of upholding international justice.

Finally, as stated in Article 115, Court assessed contributions by state parties constitute the majority of the ICC's funding. If the Court receives any funding from the UN, the General Assembly must approve of it first. Delegates of the Rome Conference also determined that they, the state parties, should be the final overseers of the Court's action. In other words, the Court is ultimately accountable to the state parties. This provides the member states with the final voice over all of the Court's actions.[29]

These concessions were tantamount to the interests of many of the P-5 members. One could speculate that the objectives achieved by the United States and the P-5 were enough to sway several key members of the original P-5 group into approving the Rome Statute. In the end, the Rome Statute received the support of several of the permanent Security Council members. The United Kingdom pledged its loyalty to the Like-Minded Group seven months before the Rome Conference primarily due to the inclusion of the Singapore compromise, relating to the role of the Security Council.

All of the P-5 nations desired a strong role for the Security Council in regard to the initiation of investigations by the ICC, while the Like-Minded Group and the CICC were pushing for a distinct separation between the two. Singapore suggested the following compromise: Instead of the ICC needing the approval of the Security Council to initiate every investigation, Singapore suggested that the Security Council could delay any investigation of the ICC if they had unanimous Council consent. This compromise was amenable to several of the P-5 members (including China, Russia, and the United Kingdom) and eventually led to the United Kingdom's defection from the P-5 and its current status as a member of the Like-Minded Group.[30]

During the negotiations at the Rome Conference, France also altered their position. Many observers believe that the Like-Minded Group's concessions are primarily responsible for their defection from the P-5. In particular, in order to gain French support of the final Statute, the Like-Minded Group agreed to include Article 124. This article allowed state parties to "opt out" of the war crimes provision for a period of seven years. With this concession in place, France went on to not only approve and sign the Statute; they were also one of the earliest ratifying states of the Rome Statute.[31]

In the end, the only permanent Security Council members to vote against the Rome Statute were the United States and China. Russia voted in favor of the Statute and eventually signed it, but at this point in time, the prospects of ratification seem dim. I have already discussed at length why the United States decided not to vote in favor of the Statute so let me now turn to the other major objector, China. In China's case, one could speculate that they were simply unconvinced of the need for an ICC. They appeared somewhat detached from the negotiations, as they are from many foreign policy issues and seemed unmoved by the moral necessity for a permanent ICC. From a liberal perspective, China did not share in the common interest of large portions of the international community to end impunity. In the end, only China and the United States remained within the once-powerful coalition of the P-5.

The numerous defections are a prime example of the cooperative effort that occurred between states in order to obtain a successful vote. There existed a common interest, ending impunity of the most heinous crimes; however, no one group of states received the perfect institutional outcome that they desired (what could be considered relative gains), but they all received some concessions (absolute gains). From a liberal perspective, this case shows how the application of the theory's core principles helps us understand a complex institutional formation process. We see how the actors involved saw the cooperative arrangement of creating an ICC as beneficial to their interests, how creating a court was an attempt to overcome the inevitability of conflict, how the interdependent nature of the system created a context in which cooperation and not conflict are viable means of fulfilling national interest, how nonstate actors like the CICC are influential, and, finally, how engaging in a cooperative arrangement like the ICC can assist the international system progress beyond the conflict-ridden system perceived by the realists. Although this is only one case, it shows the explanatory value of the theory along with its ability to understand institutional formation processes. One question students must engage throughout the remainder of this semester is how far does the value of this theory extend beyond negotiation processes such as the ICC. Can we see this theory applicable to security situations?

Economic considerations? Or other areas of international politics? With a foundational understanding of the theory, students now have a set of tools to examine the complex nature of the global system.

Wrap-Up

Here is the take-home message. Liberalism, although a fairly disparate theoretical perspective, shares the understanding that states can and will cooperate as a means to achieve their national interest and that despite the anarchical nature of the system, conflict is not inevitable. In fact, the basic conceptualization of the world through a realist lens might be empirically accurate. That is, the world is made up of self-interested actors who exist within an anarchical system. But this does not mean a war of all against all and the pursuit of interests via any means necessary. Liberalism argues that self-interested states begin to realize that they can fulfill those interests through cooperation. Why? Simply put, because states have a shared interest. Therefore, when there is a desire to promote free trade, the international community creates the World Trade Organization, and when there is a need to protect a group of like-minded states from an external threat, they create a security arrangement like NATO. What the liberals do best is question as to how so many cooperative arrangements could exist if the realist understanding of world politics was empirically accurate. The answer they provide is shared interest and cooperation as a means of achieving self-interest.

Further Reading

1. David A. Baldwin, *Neorealism and Neoliberalism: The Contemporary Debate* (1993), provides an excellent encapsulation of the neorealism-neoliberalism debate. He establishes a six-point comparative analysis of the theories (from which this chapter borrows), making it clear where the two theories overlap and where they diverge. For anyone wanting to understand the distinctions in each theory and understand how the two perspectives relate to one another and how they differ, Baldwin's text is an indispensable resource.
2. Robert O. Keohane, *After Hegemony: Cooperation and Discord in the World Political Economy* (1984), is the primary text of neoliberalism. Keohane provides a solid empirical argument for how the anarchical nature of the system can still provide for widespread cooperation. This remains the definitive counter to Waltz's *Theory of International Politics* and its neorealist premises.

3. Robert O. Keohane and Joseph Nye Jr., *Power and Interdependence: World Politics in Transition* (1977), provide a major shift in liberal theory, pushing it toward a more empirical assessment of the world, while still arguing that state cooperation is a fundamental part of the international community. The text establishes the concept of complex interdependence and its place within the study of international politics.

4. Alfred Zimmern, "Organize the World Peace" (1934), is one of the key academic arguments in favor of classical liberalism and its more "idealist" position. Zimmern believes in the possibility of peace and provides a set of first principles of policy that must be met if that peace is to remain possible. He provides a big emphasis on international law, the power of morality, and collective action.

5. Ole Waever, *The Rise and Fall of the Inter-Paradigm Debate* (1994), is an advanced engagement of what many scholars refer to as the "Third Debate." It discusses the core question about what international relations is made up of. In other words, what is the nature of international politics and how do we study this academic field. Waever bemoans the fact that the main paradigms are speaking past one another and the need for further dialogue.

Notes

[1] As stated in the introductory chapter, the intent of each chapter is to provide students with an overview of the theory, not a detailed examination of each theoretical offshoot. Therefore, although many different forms of liberalism exist, this chapter focuses on the ones that are most important to introductory students seeking a general understanding of the theory.

[2] The democratic peace theory is generally discussed as part of the liberal perspective. Although this notion that democracies do not fight democracies and, as a result, the premise that a world full of democracies would be a more peaceful place does have it theoretical roots in liberalism, this remains but one way to explain peace. Therefore, this chapter does not discuss this principle in any detail, although I anticipate that your class will engage this topic again when discussing the issue-area of conflict and security.

[3] Some scholars have also referred to idealism as liberalism, utopianism, or pluralism. It is important to note that no matter the term associated with this line of thinking, the underlying philosophical tenets are the same. During the inter-war period, idealist scholars were engaged in a theoretical debate with proponents of realist thinking. This is usually referred to as the first debate in international relations theory. For a more detailed discussion of this debate, see Steve Smith, "Self-Images of a Discipline: A Genealogy of International Relations Theory," in *International Relations Theory Today*, eds. Ken Booth and Steve Smith (University Park: The Pennsylvania University Press, 1995).

[4] The primary objective of preventing war is best exemplified in the work of Zimmern 1945. In this article, Zimmern states, "the overriding objective of policy in the present generation . . . is the prevention of war" (156).

5 Baron Charles de Secondat Montesquieu, *Spirit of the Laws* (London: Penguin Books, 1748 [reprint 2002]).

6 Immanuel Kant, *To Perpetual Peace: A Philosophical Sketch* (Indianapolis, IN: Hackett, 1795 [reprint 2003]).

7 This list is developed from the writings of numerous classical liberal scholars. This list includes: Norman Angell, *The Great Illusion: A Study of the Relations of Military Power to National Advantage* (London: William Heinemann, 1912); David Shotwell, "Alternatives for War," *Foreign Affairs* 6 (1928): 459–67; Alfred Zimmern, "Organize the Peace World," *Political Quarterly* 5 (1934): 156; Alfred Zimmern, *The League of Nations and the Rule of Law: 1918–1935* (London: MacMillan, 1945); and Leonard Woolf, "DeProfundis," *Political Quarterly* 10 (1939): 463–76. Martin Hollis and Steve Smith, *Explaining and Understanding International Relations* (Leicester, UK: Clarendon Press, 1991), 17–20 also succinctly summarize the foundational components of classical liberalism.

8 Hedley Bull, *The Anarchical Society: A Study in World Politics*, 2nd edition (New York: Columbia University Press, 1995), 34.

9 Woolf, "DeProfundis," 474–75.

10 The 1970s provided numerous challenges to the hegemonic nature of realism. Complex interdependence is one challenger. The other main challenger comes in the form of Marxist/radical writings that are discussed in a later chapter. For the sake of brevity this chapter has also skipped the functionalist phase of liberalism that is best exemplified in the work of Haas 1964 and Mitrany 1948.

11 This theory has its roots in Keohane and Nye 1971, but the bulk of this discussion is derived from Keohane and Nye 1977.

12 Robert O., Keohane and Joseph Nye Jr., *Power and Interdependence: World Politics in Transition* (Boston, MA: Little Brown, 1977), 25.

13 Keohane and Nye, *Power and Interdependence*, 13.

14 Keohane and Nye, *Power and Interdependence*, 13.

15 Robert O. Keohane, "Institutional Theory and the Realist Challenge," in *Neorealism and Neoliberalism: The Contemporary Debate*, ed. David A. Baldwin (New York: Columbia University Press, 1993), 272.

16 International relations scholars refer to neoliberal institutionalism by several different titles. These include: neoliberal, institutionalism, contractualism, functionalism, and pluralism. Despite these different terms and some nuanced differences between these perspectives, the core of their thinking remains the same and can be referred to as neoliberalism or neoliberal institutionalism.

17 Stephen Krasner, "Structural Causes and Regime Consequences: Regimes as Intervening Variables," *International Organization* 36, no. 2 (1982): 186 defines regimes as "sets of implicit or explicit principles, norms rules or decision-making procedures around which actors' expectations converge in a given issue-area."

18 Keohane, "Institutional Theory and the Realist Challenge," 271.

19 Thomas Hobbes, *Leviathan* (London: Penguin Books, 1651 [reprint 1982]), 186.

20 Robert Axelrod and Robert O. Keohane, "Achieving Cooperation under Anarchy: Strategies and Institutions," *World Politics* 38, no. 1 (1985): 226.

21 This builds on the philosophical principles of Locke 1689, among others.

22 Robert O. Keohane, *After Hegemony: Cooperation and Discord in the World Political Economy* (Princeton, NJ: Princeton University Press, 1984), 51–52.

[23] Keohane, *After Hegemony.*
[24] Keohane, *After Hegemony*, 6. Keohane also expands on this premise in his later work, Keohane, "Institutional Theory and the Realist Challenge," 274–78.
[25] It is important to remember that the prevalence of common interests does not automatically equate into cooperation. Discord can result despite the presence of common interests among states. Keohane is describing a cooperative process, not the presence of harmony. According to neoliberal institutionalists, if harmony existed there would be no need for cooperation. Keohane, *After Hegemony*, 12–13.
[26] For a more detailed discussion of hegemony see Stephen Gill, "Epistemology, Ontology, and the Italian School," in *Gramsci, Historical Materialism and International Relations*, ed. Stephen Gill (Cambridge: Cambridge University Press, 2003), 41–42.
[27] Keohane, *After Hegemony*, 50.
[28] Rome Statute of the ICC, Article 17.1-2 and Article 20. John T. Holmes, "The Principle of Complementarity," discusses the nuances of this principle at length. One important component of this principle is the fact that the decision concerning unwillingness is to be determined by a panel of three ICC judges. Thus, the ultimate power of prosecution lies with this group of individuals.
[29] Scheffer 1998 mentions fourteen objectives that the U.S. achieved. I consider the seven mentioned in this text to be the most representative.
[30] Benedetti and Washburn 1999: 19–20 and Brown 2000: 63 both discuss the compromise and the support that it received.
[31] France was the twelfth state to ratify the Rome Statute on June 9, 2000.

Works Cited

Angell, Norman. 1912. *The Great Illusion: A Study of the Relations of Military Power to National Advantage.* London: William Heinemann.
Axelrod, Robert, and Robert O. Keohane. 1985. "Achieving Cooperation under Anarchy: Strategies and Institutions." *World Politics.* 38, no. 1: 226–54.
Benedetti, Fanny, and John L. Washburn. 1999. "Drafting the International Criminal Court Treaty: Two Years to Rome and an Afterword on the Rome Diplomatic Conference." *Global Governance.* 5, no. 1: 1–37.
Brown, Bartram S. 2000. "The Statute of the ICC: Past, Present and Future." In Sarah Sewall and Carl Kaysen, eds. *The United States and the International Criminal Court: National Security and International Law.* Lanham, MD: Rowman & Littlefield.
Bull, Hedley. 1995. *The Anarchical Society: A Study in World Politics*, 2nd edition. New York: Columbia University Press.
Gill, Stephen. 2003. "Epistemology, Ontology, and the Italian School." In Stephen Gill, ed. *Gramsci, Historical Materialism and International Relations.* Cambridge: Cambridge University Press.
Haas, Ernst. 1964. *Beyond the Nation-State: Functionalism and International Organization.* Stanford, CA: Stanford University Press.
Hobbes, Thomas. 1651 (reprint 1982). *Leviathan.* London: Penguin Books.
Hollis, Martin, and Steve Smith. 1991. *Explaining and Understanding International Relations.* Leicester, UK: Clarendon Press.

Holmes, John T. 1999. "The Principle of Complementarity." In Roy S. Lee, ed. *The International Criminal Court: The Making of the Rome Statute— Issues, Negotiations, Results.* The Hague: Kluwer Law International.

Kant, Immanuel. 1795 (reprint 2003). *To Perpetual Peace: A Philosophical Sketch.* Indianapolis, IN: Hackett.

Keohane, Robert O. 1984. *After Hegemony: Cooperation and Discord in the World Political Economy.* Princeton, NJ: Princeton University Press.

Keohane, Robert O. 1993. "Institutional Theory and the Realist Challenge." In David A. Baldwin, ed. *Neorealism and Neoliberalism: The Contemporary Debate.* New York: Columbia University Press.

Keohane, Robert O., and Joseph Nye, Jr. eds. 1971. *Transnational Relations and World Politics.* Princeton, NJ: Princeton University Press.

Keohane, Robert O., and Joseph Nye, Jr. 1977. *Power and Interdependence: World Politics in Transition.* Boston, MA: Little Brown.

Krasner, Stephen. 1982. "Structural Causes and Regime Consequences: Regimes as Intervening Variables." *International Organization.* 36, no. 2: 185–205.

Locke, John. 1689 (reprint 1986). *The Second Treatise of Civil Government.* London: Penguin Books.

Mitrany, David. 1948. "The Functional Approach to World Organization." *International Affairs.* 24, no. 3: 350–63.

Montesquieu, Baron Charles de Secondat. 1748 (reprint 2002). *Spirit of the Laws.* London: Penguin Books.

Rome Statute of the International Criminal Court. 1998. https://www.icc-cpi. int/nr/rdonlyres/ea9aeff7-5752-4f84-be94-0a655eb30e16/0/rome_statute_ english.pdf.

Scheffer, David. 1998. "Development at the Rome Treaty Conference." Transcript of a speech to the Foreign Relations Committee, United States Senate. *US Department of State Dispatch.* 9: 19–23.

Shotwell, David. 1928. "Alternatives for War." *Foreign Affairs.* 6: 459–67.

Smith, Steve. 1995. "Self-Images of a Discipline: A Genealogy of International Relations Theory." In Ken Booth and Steve Smith, eds. *International Relations Theory Today.* University Park: The Pennsylvania University Press.

Woolf, Leonard. 1939. "DeProfundis." *Political Quarterly.* 10: 463–76.

Zimmern, Alfred. 1934. "Organize the Peace World," *Political Quarterly.* 5: 156.

Zimmern, Alfred. 1945. *The League of Nations and the Rule of Law: 1918– 1935.* London: MacMillan.

CHAPTER 4

Marxism

Why Social Class Matters

Eric K. Leonard

According to the World Bank, almost half the world's population, over 3 billion people, live on less than $2.50 a day, and over 80 percent live on less than $10 a day. In 2006, the world's wealthiest countries (approximately 1 billion people) accounted for 76 percent of the world's gross domestic product (GDP), but low-income countries (over 2.4 billion people) accounted for only 3.3 percent of the GDP. The United Nations Development Program (UNDP) found that more than 80 percent of the world's population lives in countries where income differentials are widening, and the poorest 40 percent of the world's population account for only 5 percent of global income while the richest 20 percent account for 75 percent of income. These types of statistics could go on and on, but they all point to one glaring fact, the world is an inequitable and discriminatory place.[1] Enter the Marxists, the one theoretical perspective that emphasizes such statistics and employs them to assist in understanding conflict, security, human rights, and all other global issues.

Marxism is the first "alternative" theory this textbook discusses. What I mean by alternative theory is one that resides outside of the mainstream paradigms of realism and liberalism. The theories discussed from this point forward all fit this description, with some making greater inroads into the mainstream debate than others, while still others wax and wane in their importance. Marxism truly fits this latter description. For this alternative perspective, there have been high and low points—times in which it seemed that the perspective was becoming more widely accepted as a means to understanding global politics and moments when it is thrown in the dustbin of theoretical history. For many IR theorists, Marxism currently lacks any theoretical relevance. The end of the Cold War meant the end of communism and subsequently the end of

Marxism. However, it is important to remember the purpose of theory—it is not a policy (although it can be used as such); it is a means by which to explain, understand, and possibly predict the relations that exist in global politics. The decline of communism as a political movement and/or as a basis for governance does not necessarily mean that Marxism has lost its ability to explain and understand the international system. Marxist scholars can achieve this despite the collapse of the Soviet Union and the embrace of many capitalist tendencies by China. In many ways, assessing the relevance of Marxism is the goal of this chapter.

Because of this confusion, the best advice I can give students embarking on an analysis of Marxist/radical thought, whether it is specific to international politics or political philosophy more broadly, is to forget everything you know about Marxism. In my years of teaching this theoretical perspective, both within the IR classroom and in political philosophy courses, it has become apparent that most students, especially American students, start with a skewed conceptualization of Marx and his ideas. As already mentioned, for those students Marxism is bound up in the now-dissolved Soviet Union, pseudo-capitalist China, or the outcast countries of North Korea, Cuba, or some other form of authoritarian rogue regime. However, the true nature of Marxism is profoundly different from these skewed realities, and the application of Marx's theoretical perspective to international politics, in some ways, has little to do with the construct of such regimes. Therefore, I would ask that you forget what you know and start your analysis of Marxism with a clean slate.

With that in mind, where do we start? This is a more difficult question than you may think. As one can see in the application of Marxism politically, it is difficult to discern what is true Marxism, or if a true or pure form of Marxism even exists. Is Marxism what we saw emerge and challenge the West during the Cold War? Is it an authoritarian-based perspective that appears antithetical to democracy, human rights, and private property? Or is it the most democratic theoretical perspective, one that challenges the hierarchical nature of the global capitalist system in an attempt to emancipate the impoverished third world masses?

Along with these questions of application, one may also talk about Marxism in disparate theoretical terms. Some of the disparate forms of Marxism include orthodox Marxism, Lenin imperialists, dependency theorists, world systems perspectives, critical theorists, or a host of other qualifying adjectives. Nevertheless, despite this disparate nature, there are certain attributes or conceptualizations of world politics that bind all Marxists together. These include a class-based analysis of the global community, a focus on historical evolution, an emphasis on the economic nature of that historical evolution without discounting the social and/ or political factors of history, an understanding of the hierarchical nature of the international system, and a normative component to the theory that desires an emancipatory conclusion to one's analysis. This chapter discusses all of these attributes first, so that students may have a foundational conceptualization of the theory, before discussing some of the more prominent neo-Marxist perspectives including Lenin's imperialism, dependency theory, and world-systems theory. Hopefully, upon completing this chapter, students will have a better understanding of Marxism and how the theory remains beneficial to our analytical toolbox.

Thinking Like a Marxist

When you look at the world, what do you see? Do you see nation-states with strong governments, clearly defined borders, and a patriotic citizenry? When thinking about your identity as it relates to global politics, do you define yourself by your nationality? Are you American, German, Chinese, Iranian, Nigerian, Brazilian, etc.? For a Marxist, such a conceptualization of society is what prevents us from truly understanding how the international system works. For them, the primary driving identity of global politics is class, more specifically economic class. For a Marxist, this identifying characteristic is the most consequential to your life—it affects you in a more definitive way than any other characteristic and is the cause of most conflict. Think about the importance that economic and social status plays in your life. Did it affect your education by limiting your choices both at the secondary and college level? Does it prevent you from ascertaining certain needs and wants? Economics is the fundamental part of our life and as long as "money makes the world go round," the Marxist critique of how the global community distributes this money and the consequences of such distribution will always remain relevant. Where you sit on the economic hierarchy is a guiding principle for your behavior. The same applies to the international system. The United States acts to maintain its position in the global economic hierarchy, and the result is a system of winners and losers. The consequences of this system are poverty, exploitation, and conflict, but it can also be revolution, change, and equality. To view the world from a Marxist perspective is to embrace this alternative viewpoint.

Foundational Principles

The divergent philosophy of Marxism centers on a basic core espoused by Karl Marx.[2] The fact that many discussions and applications of Marxism do not return to the actual writings of Marx is one of the fundamental problems in trying to assess Marxism as a theory of global politics. Therefore, this chapter initially engages students in a brief discussion of Marxism as defined by Marx. This section focuses on three core principles of Marxism: (a) The importance Marx places on dialectical materialism as a way to view history, (b) The class-based understanding of politics that results in inherent inequalities, discrimination, and eventually conflict, and (c) The emancipatory nature of Marxism and its normative desire to create a free and fair political community. Let us begin with Marx's dialectical approach and the resulting view of history.

Dialectical Materialism and History

At the core of all Marxist thought is a reliance on historical analysis; however, Marxists center this historical analysis on the economic materialist evolution of humanity.[3] When Marx analyzed the progression of humanity, he viewed it from what has become known as a historical materialist perspective. For Marx, history is a series of conflicts that occur and upon rectification move us forward. Originally derived from the philosophy of Georg Wilhelm Friedrich Hegel, this dialectical approach to understanding provided insight into the complex relations that define our world.[4]

Although a comprehensive discussion of dialectics is beyond the scope of this chapter, students should recognize that Hegel was trying to explain and understand the world by examining the interdependent relationships that define our reality. Three core principles define a dialectical approach: (a) Dialectics views the world as constantly in motion or flux. The adage, "one can never step in the same river twice," best captures this principle.[5] (b) Everything in this constantly changing system is related and has an anti-thesis or a negative that helps define that entity. Without black (thesis) there would be no white (anti-thesis), and without a slave (thesis) there would be no master (anti-thesis) are two excellent examples of this principle. (c) Finally, this process of change and interdependence is also developing and unfolding with the result being a synthesis of these related but often clashing principles.[6] Simplistically, Hegel viewed the world in terms of competing theses and anti-theses that would clash and upon rectification move us forward in our understanding to a synthesis. However, that synthesis would become a thesis with an anti-thesis that would also need to be rectified to move our understanding forward. Hegel believed that we can understand everything in the world in this manner and therefore proposed an extremely complex and comprehensive philosophical perspective.

When Marx adopts this dialectical method he makes one fundamental change to it—instead of trying to explain and understand all relationships, Marx wants to focus on the social, political, and economic relationships that define history. The result is his dialectical materialist perspective, named as such because of its focus on the materialist relationships that define each historical moment. In dialectical materialism, one views the world in terms of its social, political, and economic relationships. Marx characterizes each historical epoch by the underlying base or substructure that defines that period. The base of the society is the overarching economic relationship. The production process and those who own the means of production (the material needed to produce goods) and those who do not own the means of production define this relationship. These relations of production create antagonism between workers and owners.

According to Marx, history has had several antagonistic stages, with the base and substructure defining them all. The master–slave relationship defined the period of slavery, the lord–serf relationship defined the feudal period, and the bourgeoisie (owners) and proletariat (laborers) relationship defines the current capitalist system. Along with the base, there also exists a superstructure. The superstructure is the social institutions that serve to justify the base relations. If we think about this in terms of the current capitalist system, students should ask what institutions work to perpetuate the capitalist system. Is it the government, schools, media, or even religion? According to Marx, it is all of the above. All of these institutions, in their own way, justify and/ or perpetuate the current base economic structure thus making it more acceptable to the exploited bourgeoisie.

For example, our schools teach students about the principle of equal opportunity and perpetuate the idea that regardless of where you begin in the economic hierarchy, you can gain the same level of success as anyone else. But for a Marxist, this principle is just a myth created by the bourgeoisie to provide the proletariat with a false sense of hope. Yes, success stories do exist (the Oprah Winfreys of the world), but for every success story, there are thousands if not millions of proletariats who remain in their exploited lower class position until their impoverished demise. As a result, proletariats live their life in a state of false consciousness never recognizing the fact that because of their class identity, their exploited and impoverished position will never change.[7] They continue to cling to the hope of success while never realizing anything beyond a middle-class existence, at best.

Class-Based Identity

If you recall, this book's previously discussed IR theories focused on a particular territorial-based actor as being dominant and influential.

According to these theories, in order to understand international politics, it was necessary to focus mainly on states, but possibly also on intergovernmental organizations (IGOs), nongovernmental organizations, or individuals acting within their governmental capacity. However, with the Marxists these conceptualizations of world politics change, and the nation-state or some IGO is not the primary identity that defines the global community. As should be clear from the previous section, for Marxists the defining characteristic of all societies is class.

Marx defines class as the "social relations between the producers, and the conditions under which they exchange their activities and share in the total act of production."[8] In other words, an individual's relationship to the means of production defines their class. This is very different from a modern conceptualization of class, which usually defines class by income. Instead, Marx asserts that those who do not own the forces of production are part of the proletariat class, while the bourgeoisie are the owners. This means that the defining social relationship of production is that if the proletariat wishes to produce anything, they must borrow or purchase the means from the bourgeoisie. This places the proletariat in a conflict-laden situation with the bourgeoisie because Marx asserts that it is part of our nature to labor (not work but labor or produce something in a productive manner). In fact, this is the defining existential characteristic of our species.[9] By denying the proletariat the ability to own the means of production, it in many ways denies them a part of their humanity. The result is the exploitation of the proletariat class and eventually conflict over the means of production and the capacity to labor freely.

A New Definition of Freedom

This brings us to the final characteristic that binds all Marxists, the idea that freedom can only occur when one is able to labor freely. As mentioned above, Marx believes that all human beings want to labor. It is important to distinguish between labor and work, because for Marx, the two are fundamentally different activities. Labor is the process by which human beings create. It is the defining aspect of our humanity, and the notion of free labor is what distinguishes us from other animal species. However, capitalism does not allow the proletariat to labor freely. In a capitalist society, the proletariat must work; work is a forced activity that is necessary to sustain oneself in a capitalist system. For most of our existence we work—wake up in the morning, work for 8–10 or more hours a day, go home, eat, sleep, and get up and do it again. However, this activity of work, according to Marx, is not labor because it is not free. If you live in a capitalist society, you must work in order to survive. Which means you must sell your labor, which is what makes it work. The ultimate goal of communism is to break these alienating chains and create a society that allows individuals to labor freely.[10]

In regard to IR theory, scholars often criticize this teleological aspect of Marxism. No one can deny that Marxism has a normative goal in mind, an end if you will, that Marxists desire. They believe that the hierarchical, exploitative capitalist system is bad and we must rectify the subsequent inequalities. Thus, Marxists want to initiate change in the system. This normative perspective runs counter to what many believe a theory is supposed to do. However, before we write off Marxism as an inadequate theoretical perspective, it is important to recognize that Marx had what many consider a very empirically defensible perspective of our modern capitalist society. If theory is supposed to explain and understand a phenomenon, one could claim that Marxists perform these tasks better than most when it comes to capitalism. They even maintain the ability to provide some predictive capabilities concerning how the primary actors within capitalism will behave. They, unlike most other IR theories, take this understanding and make a normative claim about what they see. I do not believe this undermines their status as an IR theory because if one does not wish to adhere to or pursue the emancipatory nature of the theory, they can still gain a better understanding of the current and future international system.

Forms of Marxism

As with all theories, there are several different forms of Marxism. However, because Marxism is a theoretical perspective that is employed by many disciplines, it is sometimes more difficult to grasp how it applies to just one. Within the field of international politics, there have been many variations on traditional Marxist thinking. Some have remained relatively true to Marx and his writings, while some have initiated some dramatic transformations. However, in the end, they are all considered Marxist.

Imperialism and the Influence of Lenin

This perspective is probably the most widely known and acknowledged form of Marxism within the international politics literature and evolves into the modern day dependency perspective, which will be discussed further in the following section. One reason for this is that Vladimir Lenin's writings are its primary source of literature, along with the work of Nikolai Bukharin and a non-Marxist John Hobson.[11] These two prolific Marxist philosophers/writers, along with the global economic insight of Hobson's earlier work, establish a foundation for a portion of Marxist thought that probably retains the greatest application to the current international political context. The reason for this relevance is the fact that this form of Marxism makes the theory a truly global perspective, in that it discusses the notion of a socioeconomic hierarchy that exists not simply within domestic political systems, but among the community of states. This hierarchical structure creates a system in which less developed states (LDCs) become dependent on the more developed states and the multinational corporations (MNCs) that dominate these advanced industrialized countries. Thus, we see the theoretical development of Marxist thinking from imperialism to the more contemporary dependency perspective.[12]

But let's not get ahead of the story. It is important that students first comprehend the foundational principles of imperialism and how this perspective provides a solid foundation for understanding today's global system. Imperialism, as Lenin informs us, is the highest stage of capitalism. In the early twentieth century, what Lenin and others were attempting to explain is why the Marxist revolution had not yet occurred. Marx's writings were now several decades old, and those that favored a movement to a global communist revolution were wondering why the collapse of capitalism had not yet occurred. There were many opinions on this issue, but Lenin and Bukharin held one of the more widely accepted perspectives when they argued that it was the result of capitalists moving their industries beyond their national borders and into the less developed world. The decision by the industrialized states to move their industries to the less developed world (mainly outside of Western Europe) was necessitated by the need for a new means of profit. According to the theory of imperialism, if capitalists remain wedded to their own domestic markets, they will eventually create their own demise by over exploiting their proletariat and creating massive monopolies. These two factors will create declining profits (because with lower wages and less workers who is going to purchase your products), a growing proletariat (because with the increase in monopolies many of the bourgeoisie are being hurled down into the ranks of the proletariat), increased immiseration (more and more people struggling to survive in the faltering capitalist system), and eventually revolution—all of which is a very classical Marxist take on why revolution occurs.[13] What the theory of imperialism adds to Marx's teachings is a new source of labor, resources, and even markets that will slow the immiseration process and the descent toward revolution.

The movement to set up industries in the less developed world is one that all capitalists, if they hope to survive and profit, must make. This is not about free choice; it is about survival in a capitalist system. What the bourgeoisie gain from this relationship is a cheap source of labor, abundant (and inexpensive) natural resources, and, as these nation-states develop, hopefully, new markets. The result is what Lenin termed "super profits," an amount of profit that could never be garnered by simply remaining in one's domestic market. However, the importance of imperialism is not only about the dependent relationships created between the developed and the developing worlds but also about the use of super profits to quell the threat of revolution amongst the industrialized proletariat.

According to Lenin the bourgeoisie will not only use these super profits to directly benefit themselves but will also use them to perpetuate the proletariats' state of false consciousness. The way in which the bourgeoisie accomplish this placation of the proletariat is to use some of the super profits to benefit the workers in their home state or country. This use of profit creates a stabilization of the revolutionary fervor of the proletariat by making their lives economically bearable. In essence, the bourgeoisie "buy-off" the proletariat while still generating tremendous profit through the exploitation of the workers in their colonial holdings.

So for Lenin, where does revolution begin? Instead of claiming the start of a revolution in the industrialized centers of Europe, imperialists see the revolution starting in the less developed world. In addition, these revolutionary sparks will not begin as anti-capitalist, Marxist-based movements; they will begin as wars of national liberation. In other words, the start of the Marxist revolution occurs as a war of independence and a desire to throw out the colonial powers. The exploited workers in these less developed countries are more concerned with political independence than class-consciousness. Their motivation for revolution is a desire to throw out the imperialists and gain political control of their territory. But the subsequent result is a take-over of the industries and a loss of power by the bourgeoisie in this territory as well. Once the bourgeoisie loses the source of their super profits, they must return to the classical Marxist exploitation cycle. This results in the increased immiseration of the proletariat, a rise in class-consciousness in the developed world, and eventually revolution.

So where does this leave us in the twenty-first-century world, where imperialism and colonization are mainly a thing of history books? Marxists have evolved in how they understand world politics and in many ways have abandoned the notion of revolution in favor of understanding the relationships that determine behavior in global politics. This is not to say that the neo-Marxists do not desire change in the capitalist system (they do remain somewhat normative in their orientation), just that the idea of a global communist, workers of the world unite, style revolution is not the priority. Instead, they attempt to shed light on the exploitative relationships that they believe dominate the global marketplace in an attempt to emancipate the modern-day proletariat and create a more equitable market. The work of dependency theorists provides the best exemplification of this perspective.

Dependency Theory

The dependency literature takes a neo-imperialist perspective on world politics by looking at the role MNCs, foreign aid, commodity markets, international organizations (IOs), and other tools of the capitalist world powers play in the relationship between the developed industrialized world (the First World or core) and less developed world (Third World or LDCs). One of the most prolific dependency theory scholars defines dependency as a "situation in which a certain number of countries have their economy conditioned by the development and expansion of another . . . placing the dependent countries in a backward position exploited by the dominant country."[14] The result is a system in which the developed states of the world use their capitalist power and influence to exploit the less developed countries for economic, social, and political gain. The result is a global political system that prevents less developed countries from developing and maintains a dependent relationship in which the economic viability of LDCs relies on the economic viability and profitability of first world countries and MNCs. And not only is their economic viability dependent on these first world countries and institutions (MNCs and IOs like the International Monetary Fund and the World Bank) but their economic status will also always be subordinate to the first world countries. Thus, the less developed countries will always remain less developed as long as the global capitalist system remains in place. As Gunder Frank explains, "historical research demonstrates that contemporary underdevelopment is in large part the historical product of past and continuing economic and other relations between the satellite underdeveloped and the now developed metropolitan countries. Furthermore, these relations are an essential part of the capitalist system on a world scale as a whole."[15] What this means is that as long as capitalism remains the dominant model of the global economy, a system of "haves" and "have-nots" will remain. If we employ the same language as the classical Marxists, the proletariat (the less developed countries of the world) remains impoverished and immiserated, while the bourgeoisie (the developed states) flourish and profit. It is not until the developing world recognizes the exploitative relationship that exists between them and the first world that this cycle of poverty and underdevelopment can end. It is the moment of class consciousness that brings about change in the system and the end of dependency and underdevelopment. Therefore, the link back to the imperialism literature is obvious, but the ability to break the cycle of immiseration has become more complex.

However, this is not to say that no one in these less developed countries are profiting from this relationship. As the classic work of Fernando Enrique Cardoso and Enzo Faletto explains, "Development is itself a social process."[16] Thus, development within these third-world countries involves not only the relationship between the developed world and the LDCs but also the indigenous elites of these societies and the relationships that they cultivate. In other words, the dependency occurs because of the external factors discussed above along with the developing world and its actors creating a situation where internal forces also benefit relative to their current economic/social/political position. These internal forces, known as national bourgeoisie, are those that engage the bourgeoisie from the developed world, whether they are government officials or MNC representatives, and provide them national assistance in the exploitation of the less developed workers. As a result, this national bourgeoisie profits from the exploitative actions of the developed world and in fact assists in the perpetuation of the underdevelopment of the third world.

This puts a new wrinkle on Leninist imperialism and what is necessary to break the cycle and move toward revolution. According to the dependency theorists, the destruction of the national bourgeoisie must occur if the nation-state is to gain any sense of autonomous development and control over its economy and production process. Only by breaking the relations between these two capitalist entities can history move forward.

It is interesting to note that the dependency theorists are a group of neo-Marxists that do not necessarily seek a classic Marxist revolution. When reading the dependency literature, it appears that the purpose of the "revolution" is not to begin a movement toward global communism, but instead to gain autonomy of one's production process in a version of Lenin's war of national liberation. Cardoso exemplified this policy position when he became the president of Brazil, and while he did champion the plight of the poor and the underprivileged, he did not move Brazil toward a modern form of communism. Instead, he attempted to initiate a more equitable domestic society through socialist means (government-controlled programs), while also making Brazil a viable power in the global marketplace. It seems reasonable to say that Cardoso understood that gaining control of Brazil's production process would make them a more competitive economy in the global market, which would in turn benefit the domestic social, economic situation in

Brazil. However, this development needed to occur on Brazil's terms and not via the international exploitation of their natural resources or cheap labor. This may be a model for the future of Marxist thought. This entails the idea that Marxism has validity in the contemporary global political arena, not in regard to a "workers of the world unite" type revolution but in its ability to understand and explain the global inequalities that exist amongst the world's nation-states. Moreover, it establishes a policy option for third world impoverishment that the global community can act upon and possibly even allow for the rectification of some of the statistics mentioned in the opening pages of this chapter.

World-Systems Theory

World-systems theory is another form of Marxism that does not necessarily rely on a global communist revolution to justify its relevance. However, world-systems theory does continue the Marxist understanding that world politics is economically based and that the global economy is constructed of dominant political entities that use their position of power, most notably in the economic realm, to exploit those in lower positions of relative power. In other words, world-systems theory still views the world as the big guy using their strength to pick on the little guy. Along with this, world-systems theory also views capitalism as an integrated, historically expanding system that transcends any particular political or geographical boundaries. They argue that the study of global politics should not focus on individual states or national economies but should focus on the system as a whole and the distribution of power in that system, which results from the economic order that exists at that time. The result is the study of two distinct but interrelated subsystems— the global economy, which is driven by capital accumulation, and the state system, which is defined by the political and military distribution of power. The key to understanding the world system is the recognition that the economic system determines the political/military system.

The primary author of world-systems theory is Immanuel Wallerstein. In Wallerstein's words,

A world system is a social system, one that has boundaries, structures, member groups, rules of legitimation and coherence. Its life is of the conflicting forces that hold it together by tension and tear it apart as each group seeks eternally to remold it to its advantage. It has the characteristics of an organism, in that it has a life-span over which its characteristics change in some respects and remain stable in others ... Life within it is largely self-contained, and the dynamics of its development are largely internal.[17]

So in regard to Wallerstein applying this to the study of world politics, he views the international system as one in which the market drives the world and nation-states exist in an interdependent but unequal position—interdependent in that the big global economy ties all of these nation-states together, and in fact these nation-states need each other to survive and prosper and unequal in that there is a distinct hierarchy to the global society, but that inequality is not static—changes can and will occur to this power structure.

If we stick with the premise of hierarchy, Wallerstein depicts the system as having distinct categories for nation-states—the core, semiperiphery, and periphery. The relationship between the core and the periphery being the most important for understanding world politics, the semi-periphery is simply a buffer zone between the core and periphery that embodies some characteristics of each. The core includes the industrialized "northern" countries of the global community—primarily the United States, Canada, and Western Europe. These countries are capital-intensive economies where most of the wealth resides. On the other end of the spectrum is the periphery—those underdeveloped states sitting in the "south" of the global community. Most political economy scholars consider the bulk of Africa as part of the periphery. These nation-states are poor, labor-intensive economies that struggle to provide for their population.

The key to Wallerstein's analysis is not to view the two groups separately, but to view the relationship that exists amongst these actors. Remember, the world system is not only hierarchical but also interdependent. So, what is the relationship? To use the Marxist terms, the core is the bourgeoisie and the periphery is the proletariat. Thus, the core nation-states, those of western Europe and the United States, exploit the periphery, the under-developed world, for their cheap labor and abundant natural resources. The result is the continued dominance of the core, both economically and politically/militarily, and the continued underdevelopment of the periphery.

It is important to note that world-systems theorists do not see the distribution of power as static. There is a fluidity that exists amongst the world's nation-states; therefore, powers will rise, and powers will fall. The best way to see this is in Wallerstein's discussion of hegemony.[18] A hegemonic system occurs when one state simultaneously dominates the global processes of capital accumulation and the global balance of military power. A hegemon is simply a country that has the capability, and the desire, to dominate the global system. Due to the Marxist nature of world-systems theory, Wallerstein puts the greatest emphasis on the economic side of global dominance, because as stated above, that will lead to dominance in other areas. Therefore, this theory argues that as the distribution of wealth and power in the global economy shifts, so too will the hegemonic status. These long cycles of hegemonic power are one way that we can map the world system and its fluid power structure. It is also a way to see the world through a Marxist lens of winners and losers and understand that the power structure of the system is intricately tied to the economic development of the state.

Putting It All Together: Marxism and Security

How does all of this translate to an understanding of security issues as they relate to global politics? As stated earlier, all Marxists view issues of security and conflict as ultimately dependent on the economic relationships of the situation. As a result, when analyzing a security issue or the initiation of conflict, Marxist would always point to an underlying economic reason for actor behavior. Take the first Gulf War as a prime example.[19]

In 1990, Iraq, under the leadership of Saddam Hussein, decided to invade Kuwait to take control of their oil fields. Now the neorealists would have you believe this invasion was the result of the anarchical structure of the system and that, in fact, war is inevitable. The neoliberals might accept the structural rationale for the invasion but can see a diplomatic, cooperative means by which to resolve the issue because of complementary interests. However, the Marxists would see the primary cause for both invasion and reaction as economics, with the resulting war being less about ideology or nationalism and more about class and economic control.

The conflict begins with Iraq's invasion of Kuwait and subsequent occupation of that territory, so let us start with the reasons as to why Iraq invaded Kuwait in the summer of 1990. Some of the reasons given for this occupation related to historical claims over territory and the illegitimacy of the colonial borders. Although they could be reasonable claims for invasion and subsequent occupation, the Marxists would argue that such claims were secondary to the real reason—economics! Two economically based claims for Iraq's occupation of Kuwait emerge at the outset of this conflict: (a) the need for strategic access to the Gulf. This need for access to the Gulf was important in terms of exports and imports, and the future viability of Iraq's economy. (b) Iraq's need for economic stability and the rectification of its economic grievances with the rest of the Arab world.

From a Marxist perspective, what would cause the United States to build such a robust coalition and engage what many perceived at the time as an extremely powerful military force in open combat? Again, it is the economics of the situation that best explains and understands U.S. action. President Bush stated that U.S. policy in the Kuwait occupation had four objectives: (a) "the immediate, complete and unconditional withdrawal of all Iraqi forces from Kuwait," (b) "the restoration of Kuwait's legitimate government," (c) "[the] stability of Saudi Arabia and the Persian Gulf," and (d) "the protection of American citizens abroad."[20] The main rationale behind these objectives, according to the Marxist perspective, was economically driven. One thing that students should be careful of when applying these theories to real-world events is being too narrow sighted in your application. Did the United States have diplomatic reasons for wanting Iraq out of Kuwait? Such as the need to uphold Bush's New World Order? Or to defend the basic principles of the UN Charter? Yes—even a Marxist would acknowledge these other reasons. However, according to Marxist theory, the dominant reason for intervention in this dispute is economics. Therefore, the Marxist would not discount the other possible reasons, but they see them as secondary. The primary reason for the U.S. reaction was the vulnerability of the world's oil supplies that Iraq's occupation created.

With the occupation of Kuwait, Saddam Hussein's Iraq controlled 20 percent of the world's known oil reserves. If Iraq were able to extend that occupation into neighboring Saudi Arabia, they would control 40 percent of the oil reserves. With the export of Kuwaiti oil, Saddam would also gain some $20 million in profits; and this is on top of the profits he was already ascertaining from the export of Iraqi oil. In short, the occupation of Kuwait placed Iraq in a position of economic power and possible regional dominance, while also placing the world's oil consumers in a position of peril because of Saddam's control over such large amounts of oil reserves. In the end, it became apparent to not only the United States but also to large portions of the global community that the Iraq occupation must be halted and reversed.[21] Thus, the notion that a threat to oil will cause a swift and decisive reaction proved true, and it is the Marxists who have always understood that these type of economic threats are what cause behavior in global politics, even in the world of security and conflict.

Putting It All Together: Marxism and Political Economy

International Political Economy (IPE), of course, is the issue area that is truly in the Marxist's wheelhouse. IPE is what Marxists are most interested in because according to the Marxists, IPE is the underlying cause of all behavior. When thinking about the world and trying to explain and understand the behavior of actors in the world, Marxists always bring it back to the economy. As just noted, in issues of conflict and security, political economy remains the underlying cause. One can make the same argument for human rights and environmental issues. Therefore, it is imperative that we take some time to briefly examine a case study in which IPE is the focus because it will allow us to see how many other issues this affects.

Next time you are in class or walking around campus, look down and check out everyone's sneakers. I am sure you will see a nice diversity of "kicks" around campus, but I am also sure you will see a whole lot of Nikes. Everyone loves Nike! When I was a kid, it was all about getting a pair of Air Jordan's (yes Jordan's were part of Nike, not their own entity). My youngest son just begged me for a pair of KDs for his birthday. And all my kids play soccer and they love the Nike Magista, Mercurial, Hypervenom, and Tiempo cleats. Nike—a good old American success story! Born and bred at the University of Oregon by Phil Knight—kind of. Nike emerged from Knight's relationship with a couple of Japanese shoe companies in the 1960s. The origins of Nike are closely linked to the Onitsuka shoe company that sold the Tiger brand running shoe. Phil Knight initially sold these shoes but eventually emerged from this initial foray into importing running shoes with the legendary swish and the Nike Corporation was born.[22]

However, Nike was not simply an American corporation. Nike shoes were not manufactured here in the United States; instead, everything was outsourced to less developed countries. One of the first steps Knight took was to alter the primary distributing center from Japan, a more developed and expensive country, to South Korea. Eventually, Nike moved the bulk of their production to poor Asian countries, including Thailand, Indonesia, the Philippines, and Vietnam. Ultimately, this production model, although successful in terms of profit, resulted in allegations of Nike sweatshops and the violation of workers' basic human rights. Several human rights organizations alleged that workers' pay was below a necessary wage to sustain themselves and their families, and the working conditions were unsafe. Nike claimed that since they did not own the factories, they were not responsible for the human rights violations. They also claimed that their subcontractors in these impoverished nations were actually providing a way out of poverty for the indigenous population. The Nike Index, as some refer to it, tracks the level of development in a country by the activity of Nike. Thus, the Nike Index ties the development progress in these less developed countries to the production facilities of Nike Corporation. However, the critics claim that Nike is simply exploiting the population for its cheap labor and loose labor laws in order to increase their profits and benefit the developed world by providing marketable shoes at a cheaper price.

Marxist would have a field day analyzing this case because it appears to be an exemplification of how they understand the world around us and what causes actors' behavior. First and foremost, Marxists would view the actors in this case not as states, MNCs, and/or individuals but as members of a broader socioeconomic class. Nike, although a multinational corporation, is an exemplification of the bourgeoisie class and will act in the interest of maximizing their profits at the expense of the proletariat (the workers in the third world countries). From a Leninist perspective, one can also see the global economy at work and how the bourgeoisie (MNCs in the developed world) is finding ways to maximize profits by exploiting those in the less developed world. Overall, the Marxists can explain, understand, and predict the behavior of the Nikes of the world, along with those that they exploit.

Wrap-Up

Here is the take-home message. The key to understanding Marxism is in rethinking one's identity in the world. Do not think of yourself as American, Chinese, German, or any other nationality; you must think of yourself in terms of economic class. It is important to understand where you sit within the global economic hierarchy and how this affects your "freedom" and how that notion of freedom exists in the ability to labor freely. What a Marxist seeks is both the ability to better understand the world and its exploitative nature and the ability to emancipate the proletariat from their suppressed state. This distinguishes Marxism from the mainstream IR theories but does not diminish its comprehension of the world capitalist system. And although the global communist revolution has not occurred, this fact does not lessen the relevance of this theory. Its explanatory power, understanding of global political-economic relations (in particular the production process and actors' relationship to that process), and predictive capability of actors' behaviors make this theory a viable part of any IR student's toolbox for the foreseeable future.

Further Reading

1. Karl Marx, *Economic and Philosophic Manuscripts* (1844), provides the initial description of alienated labor and how alienation hinders the human species from fulfilling its innate desire to labor. Marx also provides a scathing critique of Hegelian dialectics and the need for

any dialectical understanding of the world to provide a means of change and not just understanding.

2. V. I. Lenin, *Imperialism: The Highest Stage of Capitalism* (1917), is a necessary read for anyone hoping to make sense of the current neo-imperialist debates. Lenin provides the initial understanding of why the first world would want to colonize and the benefits accrued from this. He is also one of the initial revolutionary voices calling for wars of national liberation and the overthrow of capitalism in the developing world.

3. Vincent Ferraro, "Dependency Theory: An Introduction" (2008), provides a short easy introduction to dependency theory and its applicability to our current global community. In a literature filled with jargon and difficult analytical premises, Ferraro provides an accessible understanding of the theories intellectual roots, basic premises, and current policy implications.

4. Jonathan Joseph, *Marxism and Social Theory* (2006), is an excellent introduction to Marxist thought for anyone looking to understand its broader philosophical implications. This text is not specifically focused on IR theory but does provide an accessible introduction to the basic ideas that are central to the discussions in this chapter.

5. Robert W. Cox, "Social Forces, States and World Orders: Beyond International Relations Theory" (1981), is a key part of the critical theory literature. Although critical theory is not exclusively Marxist, it does grow out of the Marxist literature and attempts to question the validity of mainstream IR theory. Cox focuses on the process of historical change and the dialectical nature of world politics in an attempt to institute a problem-solving theory. Although a difficult read, Cox is important because, in many ways, his work embodies Marx's call for philosophy to serve the purpose of changing the world.

Notes

[1] Anup Shah, "Global Poverty and Stats" provides a large number of sourced statistics on this issue (http://www.globalissues.org/article/26/poverty-facts-and-stats).

[2] All of Marx's writings are contained in Karl Marx, *Selected Writings*. In the footnotes, I will list the specific writing that can be found in the aforementioned text.

[3] Marx, *The German Ideology*, provides a robust discussion of historical materialism.

[4] G. W. F. Hegel, *Introduction to Philosophy of History* (Indianapolis, IN: Hackett, 1820 [reprint 1988]).

[5] This phrase is credited to the Greek philosopher Heraclitus.

[6] Hegel never uses the terms thesis, anti-thesis, and synthesis, but its application has been accurately employed to capture the dialectical process.

[7] For a discussion of false consciousness see Marx, *The German Ideology* and *Economic and Philosophic Manuscripts*.

[8] Marx, *Capital: A Critique of Political Economy, Volume 1*.

[9] For a discussion of our species-being see Marx, *Economic and Philosophic Manuscripts*.

[10] For a discussion of alienation see Marx, *Economic and Philosophic Manuscripts*.

[11] Lenin 1917 is generally considered the most important work on imperialism, with Bukharin 1916 as another key theoretical source. John A. Hobson's earlier work (1902) provides a non-Marxist perspective on the topic.

[12] Cardoso and Faletto 1979 is one of the foundational writings on this theory.

[13] Marx, *Capital*.

[14] Theotonio dos Santos, 1970. "La crisis del desarollo, las realciones de depndencia in America Latina," in *La Dependencia politico-economica de America Latina*, H Jaguaribe et al., eds., 180. Cited in J. Samuel Valenzeula and Arturo Valenzuela, "Modernization and Dependency: Alternative Perspectives in the Study of Latin American Underdevelopment," *Comparative Politics* 10, no. 4 (1978): 544.

[15] Andre Gunder Frank, "The Development of Underdevelopment," in *Dependence and Underdevelopment*, James D. Cockcroft, Andre Gunder Frank, and Dale Johnson, eds. (Garden City, NY: Anchor Books, 1972), 3.

[16] Frank, "The Development of Underdevelopment," 8.

[17] Immanuel Wallerstein, *The Modern World System* (New York: Academic Press, 1974), 347.

[18] Immanuel Wallerstein, "Three Instances of Hegemony in the History of the Capitalist World-Economy," *International Journal of Comparative Sociology* XXIV, no. 1–2 (1983): 100–8.

[19] The bulk of this discussion comes from Diamond 1996.

[20] This list comes from the transcript of Bush's speech on August 8, 1990.

[21] The overwhelming passage of the plethora of United Nations Resolutions, beginning with Resolution 660, verifies the global desire to end the occupation.

[22] See Clancy 2000 for a more detailed history of the Nike Corporation.

Works Cited

Bukharin, Nikolai. 1916 (reprint 1972). *Imperialism and World Economy*. London: Martin Lawrence.

Bush, George H. W. 1990. "August 8, 1990: Address on Iraq's Invasion of Kuwait." https://millercenter.org/the-presidency/presidential-speeches/august-8-1990-address-iraqs-invasion-kuwait.

Cardoso, Fernando Henrique, and Enzo Faletto. 1979. *Dependency and Development in Latin America*. Oakland: University of California Press.

Clancy, Michael. 2000. "Sweating the Swoosh: Nike, the Globalization of Sneakers and the Question of Sweatshop Labor." Georgetown University Institute for the Study of Diplomacy.

Cox, Robert W. 1981. "Social Forces, States and World Orders: Beyond International Relations Theory." *Millennium: Journal of International Studies.* 10, no. 2: 126–55.

Diamond, Howard. 1996. "The One Hundred-Hour War." Washington, DC: Georgetown University Institute for Diplomacy.

dos Santos, Theotonio. 1970. "La crisis del desarollo, las realciones de depndencia in America Latina." In H Jaguaribe et al., eds. *La Dependencia politico-economica de America Latina*, 180. Cited in Valenzeula, J. Samuel, and Arturo Valenzuela. 1978. "Modernization and Dependency: Alternative Perspectives in the Study of Latin American Underdevelopment." *Comparative Politics.* 10, no. 4: 544.

Ferraro, Vincent. 2008. "Dependency Theory: An Introduction." In Georgio Secundi, ed. *The Development Economics Reader.* London: Routledge.

Frank, Andre Gunder. 1972. "The Development of Underdevelopment." In James D. Cockcroft, Andre Gunder Frank, and Dale Johnson, eds. *Dependence and Underdevelopment.* Garden City, NY: Anchor Books.

Hegel, G. W. F. 1820 (reprint 1988). *Introduction to Philosophy of History.* Indianapolis, IN: Hackett.

Hobson, John A. 1902 (reprint 2005). *Imperialism: A Study.* New York: Cosimo.

Lenin, V. I. 1917 (reprint 1939). *Imperialism: The Highest Stage of Capitalism.* New York: International.

Marx, Karl. 1994. *Selected Writings*, Lawrence H. Simon, ed. Indianapolis, IN: Hackett.

Shah, Anup. "Global Poverty and Stats." http://www.globalissues.org/article/26/poverty-facts-and-stats.

Wallerstein, Immanuel. 1974. *The Modern World System.* New York: Academic Press.

Wallerstein, Immanuel. 1983. "Three Instances of Hegemony in the History of the Capitalist World-Economy." *International Journal of Comparative Sociology.* XXIV, no. 1–2: 100–8.

CHAPTER 5

Social Constructivism

The Power of Ideas and Norms

Alice D. Ba and Matthew J. Hoffmann

Social constructivism is now the main theoretical challenger to established perspectives within the discipline of international relations (IR). This approach to world politics rose to prominence as an alternative to the dominant paradigms by challenging their positions on the nature of the international system, the nature of actors within it, and indeed the nature of social/political interaction in general. The social constructivist focus on the role of ideas, identities, and norms offers a way to explain change in world politics, a noted weakness of mainstream approaches like realism and liberalism. The importance of social constructivism in and for the discipline of IR has, by now, been well established. However, the ability of undergraduates to grasp and understand this theoretical perspective remains problematic. Most of the articles on this perspective are too scholarly for a theoretically inexperienced undergraduate audience, while "social constructivist" sections in textbooks tend to be merely thumbnail sketches tacked on (perhaps as an afterthought) to the "main" theoretical approaches to world politics. Clearly, striking the right balance between scholarly rigor and an appropriate level of presentation is difficult, but the insights into world politics offered by constructivist thought make it imperative that such efforts are made. So, in this chapter students are offered a broad synthesis of the main tenets of social constructivism (with as little jargon as possible) and a discussion of how constructivism approaches patterns and phenomena of world politics. This discussion is framed by comparing constructivism with the generally statist treatment that topics receive in mainstream IR as exemplified theoretically by realism and liberalism.[1] Drawing on established work in the social constructivist literature, our objective is not to break new theoretical ground or offer a new empirical case, nor is it to capture all the nuances and internal debates within constructivism. Instead, this chapter is designed to provide supporting material for introducing social constructivism to an introductory international politics audience.

The placement of this chapter is ideal because it comes after students have been exposed to realism and liberalism, thus enabling them to fully grasp how social constructivism is different. Similarly, we provide simplified case studies to demonstrate social constructivist explanations. We draw from particular authors who have applied social constructivism to some prominent "real world" cases—the emergence and strengthening of the European Union, U.S. policy toward South African apartheid, and the chemical weapons ban. These are not comprehensive case studies; rather they are designed to give students a taste of how social constructivism works in practice.[2]

The chapter begins with a discussion of the main principles of social constructivist thought: the interdependent relationship between actors and their social context, and the power of ideas. The chapter then introduces three empirical examples and through them discusses four crucial aspects of social constructivism: the permissiveness of anarchy, the role of norms, the role of identity, and the role of power. The chapter's conclusion offers readers a "take-home" message about social constructivism that summarizes its main arguments.

Thinking Like a Constructivist

Consider how you may act or think differently depending on whom you are with or what situation you are in. Do you act and think differently when in a large lecture class than you do in a small discussion group? Do you assume a different identity when surrounded by friends than you do in a group of strangers or among professors?

Would you ever wear a light blue leisure suit to class? It is likely (although some of you may have a stunning fashion sense) that you would not even consider this a possibility. It is the idea of what is fashionable that constrains what you even consider possible to wear. In the 1970s, however, you would have been the "height of cool" if you wore a light blue leisure suit. What changed is not the suit, but your social context (in this case fashion norms).

Fifty years ago society expected men to ask women out on dates (rather than the other way around). The power of this rule was enhanced every time a man asked out a woman; moreover, whenever a woman did not ask out a man, it affirmed the woman's identity as passive and the man's as active. However, over time, when more women started asking out men, these actions altered the social context making it now entirely acceptable for a woman to ask a man out on a date.

All of these things exemplify the social constructivist perspective and how this theory is at play in your everyday lives. We now need to take this everyday perspective and apply it to the realm of global politics to see how different the world can appear when employing the social constructivist lens. What students will soon realize is that the world is what we make of it and the world also makes us.

Foundational Principles

The world of the twenty-first century is a very different world from that of a century ago. Some changes have been obvious. Technological and scientific revolutions have made the world both a larger and smaller place. It is larger in the sense that the world's population has quadrupled over the last century and the number of states in world politics has increased fivefold; smaller in the sense that we can communicate with and visit people and places all over the world faster than ever before. In addition, world politics has seen a geographical shift from Europe-centered politics to global politics. Other changes have been subtler. Different actors are now playing a large part in world politics, and the important issues of world politics are changing. Today the forces of globalization are transforming world politics, which has caused new issues to emerge as crucial and enabled new kinds of actors that need neither territory nor government to be part of "world politics." Political phenomena and the stuff of world politics—actors, behaviors, outcomes, and patterns—do not remain static.

All IR theories contain ideas about the nature of actors in world politics, the nature of the context that surrounds those actors, and the nature of the interactions between actors. These are necessary assumptions used for explaining why events occur and why actors choose to behave the way they do. Neorealism, for instance, maintains very clearly that the actors in world politics are power-seeking, security-conscious states. These states exist in an anarchical context where material resources (guns and money) are the most important characteristics, and they interact (mainly) competitively with each other.[3] Neoliberalism also describes the context of world politics as anarchic but differs from realism in important ways. Neoliberals ascribe importance to actors other than states (especially IOs), and they are less pessimistic about the effects of anarchy—they see cooperation being possible when IOs can help states achieve mutual interests. Ultimately, however, neither neorealism nor neoliberalism pays significant attention to ideational factors. To these theories, ideational factors are either insignificant or a means to other ends.[4]

Social constructivism is no different in terms of having ideas about actors, context, and interactions in world politics, but social constructivists have very different notions about them and therefore very different explanations for phenomena in world politics.[5] It is because of these different notions that constructivism can explain changes like those mentioned above. In order to clarify this point, let us look at actors, context, and interactions in turn.

Actors

First, social constructivists share with liberals the view that there exist wide ranges of actors who are important players in world politics. They take IOs, nongovernmental organizations, MNCs, and social movements (among others) seriously in addition to states.

Second, social constructivists claim that the interests and identities of actors in world politics are malleable; their interests and identities depend on the context in which they find themselves. This is a significant contrast with neorealists and neoliberals who consider that actors have a more or less fixed nature; states always have been and will always be self-interested—security-conscious and power-hungry according to neorealists and rational and concerned with maximizing absolute gains for neoliberals. Constructivists argue that it is better to consider that actors in world politics are dynamic, that the identity and interests of states (and other actors) change across contexts and over time. Who the actors are and what actors want is determined by their interactions with other actors and by the larger social context in which they exist. At times, some states will be security-conscious and power-hungry, not because there is something inherent about states that makes them this way but rather because states learn to be this way by interacting with other states within a specific historical context. At other times and in other contexts, interactions can lead states to have different identities, interests, and behaviors.

Social constructivists argue that states can learn to want things other than power and economic efficiency—state interests can change. States today seem to have an interest in supporting human rights, where they did not have this interest one hundred years ago. States can learn to act in ways other than competitively—state behavior can change. In Europe, states that were fighting bloody wars during the early to mid-twentieth century have now joined in a cooperative union. States can even learn to be different—state identity can change. The United States today is very different from the United States one hundred years ago. According to constructivists, the social context in which actors exist and the interactions that they have with other actors shape many of these changes.

Context

Social constructivists claim that it is impossible to describe the nature of actors independent from a particular historical context. But what characteristics define this context? While sharing with traditional approaches the assumption that the international context in which actors find themselves is anarchical, social constructivists subscribe to a much more circumscribed definition of anarchy. For social constructivists, anarchy simply means that there is no overarching authority in world politics that can make and enforce rules. Unlike traditional approaches, social constructivists do not claim that anarchy has an inherent logic of suspicion and competition nor does it result in a fixed set of consequences or resulting behavior pattern.

In addition, where traditional approaches focus on the material characteristics of the international context—the distribution of guns and money—social constructivists emphasize the social character of international life. They claim that the important aspects of the international system are its societal and ideational characteristics—ideas, rules, institutions, and meanings. Actors do not just look around at the material capabilities of their neighbors nor do they simply perform cost/benefit analysis when deciding what their behavior is going to be. Instead, actors are also influenced by their social context—shared rules, meanings, and ideas. Notions of what is right or wrong, feasible or infeasible, indeed possible or impossible, are all a part of an actor's social context, and it is these *ideas* that shape what actors want, who actors are, and how actors behave.[6]

The context of world politics is malleable. The ideas and meanings that shape actors are not static but instead change over time as actors themselves change because it is the very behavior and interactions of actors that create the ideational context of world politics. Sovereignty provides an excellent example. The rules that make up sovereignty form a crucial part of the international context in which world politics takes place. These rules shape who some actors are (states are in part defined by being sovereign), they shape some of what states want (sovereignty gives states an interest in protecting their borders), and they shape how states behave (states create customs offices, diplomatic protocols, immigration policies, and have other policies because of sovereignty). Thus, sovereignty, as a set of ideas about how to organize world politics, shapes actors. But sovereignty itself has changed and continues to change as history unfolds; the rules of sovereignty have undergone numerous changes (from absolute sovereignty to popular sovereignty for one) and they continue to evolve today (according to some, globalization and humanitarian interventions have begun to erode the power of the

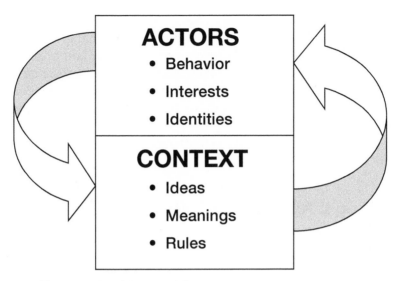

Figure 5.1 The Interaction of Actors and Context

rules of sovereignty).[7] These changes occur through the actions and interactions of actors.

Actions and Interactions

At this point, we have come full circle with constructivist thought (see figure 5.1). Actors shape their own social context and the social context, in turn, shapes the actors (interests, identities, and behaviors) themselves. This cycle is the core notion of constructivism. The actions and interactions of the actors keep the cycle moving.

Let us return to the sovereignty example. Sovereignty is a set of rules that tells state actors how to interact with one another—the rules shape actors' identities, interests, and behaviors. But the power of these rules (indeed the very existence of the rules) depends on actors acting and interacting in accordance with them. If states stop acting as though borders are inviolate, some of the rules of sovereignty will cease to have power and may cease to exist. Actors create their own common understandings—their social context—through their actions and interactions. Human rights provide another example. There is no central authority that has decreed that states should protect human rights, but the idea that it is right to protect them has come to shape the interests and behavior of many states. For example, every time a state acts to protect human rights, such as when states around the world condemned South African apartheid, it enhances the notion that it is appropriate for states to protect human rights.

Social constructivism is more complicated than other perspectives precisely because it assumes constant dynamism and change. The natures of actors and the international context are not simple and preordained. Instead, what actors do and how they interact determines the nature of the social context. In turn, this social context shapes who the actors are, what they want, and how they behave. Social constructivists claim that it is this cycle that recurs through time in world politics. It is this cycle that is the foundation of constructivist explanations of phenomena in world politics.

Putting It All Together I: The European Union[8]

There are a number of ways to approach the puzzle that the European Union (EU) presents. Traditional approaches (realism and liberalism) treat the EU as a way that states cope with what they see as the enduring, unchanging logic of anarchy. This logic of anarchy—there is no force to prevent a state from attacking or double-crossing another so all must be concerned about their own security and well-being—defines the international system and serves as the main constraint faced by states. However, the persistence and growing strength of the EU does not fit with this characterization of the international system.

Beyond the Security Dilemma: Constructing Anarchy

Realists argue that states ignore their logic of anarchy at their peril and that this logic forces states to feel insecure and to work to maintain a favorable power balance with other states in order to survive. According to realists, anarchy forces states to be security-conscious and suspicious of other states, because if they are not, they face elimination from the system. They predict recurring warfare, constant war preparation, and fleeting alliances.

In many eras of history, realists appear to be right to rely on their logic of anarchy. War, suspicion, and competition have indeed pervaded the modern international system. However, the EU today stands in stark contrast to realist predictions. These Western European states have historically been at odds, and the two world wars resulted from competition and suspicion on the continent. Yet, today, the EU unites much of Europe. Borders have disappeared between countries that once fought bloody wars. Much of Western Europe uses a common currency. All of Western Europe is a common market. How, if the realist logic of anarchy is at work, did we get from world wars to an EU?

Constructivists answer this question by arguing that the logic of anarchy at the heart of realist treatments is not set in stone. In a seminal article, Alexander Wendt makes the claim that anarchy, rather than being characterized by an unchanging logic, is what states make of it.[9] In essence, this means that anarchy is merely a permissive condition—it lacks an inherent logic. Whether anarchy forces states to be insecure and suspicious or whether it allows states to be cooperative and friendly depends on the social interactions that states have. Anarchy does not mean chaos—there are a number of rules and ideas that shape what anarchy means—nor does it imply competition. Instead, an anarchic system is filled with rules and ideas that emerge from the actions and interactions of states in the international system. If states act as if other states are potential enemies, then anarchy will lead to insecurity. If, however, states act as if other states are friends, then anarchy can lead to cooperation and trust.

Constructivists claim that this is exactly what has occurred in Western Europe since World War II. Indeed, one observer argues, "Fear of anarchy and its consequences encouraged key international actors to modify their behavior with the goal of changing that structure."[10] To be sure, the EU did not begin as an attempt to alter the logic of anarchy. At the end of World War II, two goals were uppermost in the minds of the victorious allies: (a) defend Western Europe from the Soviet Union and communism and (b) contain/control Germany. Numerous initiatives were designed to meet these two goals including the Marshall Fund, the International Bank for Reconstruction and Development (which would later become the World Bank), NATO, and the European Coal and Steel Commission. The last, and seemingly least relevant of these, would rise to become the European Community and then the EU, an organization that has altered the map and destiny of Europe as well as our understanding of IR.

However, all of these measures began for reasons that realists find very familiar—Western Europe was vulnerable, suspicious of the Soviet Union, and wary of the possibility that Germany could rise again as an aggressive power. Thus, the actions taken by the Western European states (aided, supported, and encouraged by the United States) appear to be very realist in nature. These states faced an uncertain, insecure international context and took actions to increase their security. Yet, an increase in security was not the only result of the activities that began at the close of World War II.

The Western European powers began to change their behavior toward more cooperative relations. This was not a big leap for France and Britain as they had been allies in the two world wars, but the cooperation included their enemies from the war, Germany and Italy, as well. Cooperative behavior in economic, political, and military areas, driven by the common Soviet threat, began to build trust. Beginning with the Coal and Steel Commission, the European states expanded cooperation into multiple areas of politics and economics, forming the European Court of Justice, the European Commission on Human Rights, the Organization for Security Cooperation in Europe, and the Monetary Union among others. Sustained cooperative interaction over time led to habits of cooperation, consultation, and community. States in Western Europe began to treat each other as friends. This altered the nature of anarchy. States in Western Europe turned anarchy into a cooperative structure to the point of eliminating borders between them.

At no time was this more evident than after the Cold War ended. In 1989, as the Berlin Wall fell, and in the early 1990s, when the Soviet Union dissolved and Germany reunited, Western Europe faced two realities. First, the common threat of the last forty years disappeared. Second, Germany, the feared aggressor in the world wars, was unified. What was the reaction? Did the states of Europe revert to suspicious, competitive relations and turn to individual security-building efforts, as the realist logic of anarchy would predict?[11]

No. Instead, the integration of states into the EU deepened. Through their interactions, Western European states have altered their own context. By acting cooperatively, they built trust and altered the range of possible actions and the rules governing their relations. As Emanuel Adler argues, Europe has become a security community, which means that it is "not merely a group of states that, thanks to increased communication, have abandoned war as a means of social intercourse"; it is also "a community-region in which people have mastered the practice of peaceful change."[12] Indeed, as Lebow puts it, in Europe, "the allegedly inescapable consequences of anarchy have been largely overcome by a complex web of institutions that govern interstate relations and provide mechanisms for resolving disputes."[13] Where once states fought to the death, there are now no military plans by one Union member toward another. Indeed, a common security policy and even a security community are possible today, where before they were impossible. The states of Western Europe constructed their own (cooperative) context through their actions and interactions. They escaped the realist logic of anarchy and made Europe into a zone of peace.

Beyond Cheating: Constructing European Political Order

Neoliberals agree with the realists that anarchy is an obstacle for states, but perhaps it is a smaller obstacle than realists think. Neoliberals assume that states have many mutual interests (economic gains from trade and cooperation being among the most important). Rather than ensuring constant, deadly competition, neoliberals claim that anarchy makes it difficult for states to achieve these interests because without an authority to enforce rules, cheating on "deals" will be rampant, and uncertainty will make cooperation difficult. The neoliberals claim that the EU, and other organizations, play a crucial role in helping states to overcome this fear of cheating.[14] As Peter Katzenstein argues, "These institutions facilitate monitoring, enhance political transparency, reduce uncertainty, and increase policy relevant information."[15] The EU helps the states of Europe reach mutual interests by facilitating communication and providing a set of enforceable rules that ease the fear of cheating. Put another way, international institutions can help direct state behavior in cooperative, as opposed to competitive, directions.

Thus, the transformation of Europe poses less of a problem for neoliberal approaches in that they see interstate cooperation, especially surrounding economic issues, as likely. Moreover, states will continue to value institutions like the EU even if the circumstances that brought them together in the first place (e.g., the Soviet threat) have changed. Nevertheless, neoliberal approaches are also limited, not because what they describe does not take place in the EU but because they do not capture *all* that is taking place. In particular, they do not consider the possibility that state identities and interests can change. Britain is currently a good example of the dynamism of state identities and interests. With Britain's move toward Brexit, it seems that the neoliberal ability to explain British behavior is limited. However, social constructivism captures the notion of change and can understand the reason for Brexit. What we must keep in mind is that social constructivism is a theory of continuity and change and, as a result, can capture the transformation of international politics—including a change in state's interests, identity, context, and the interaction among all of these principles.

The neoliberal views of anarchy also prevent them from seeing how international institutions are themselves a kind of social environment—not simply a set of "material rewards and punishments," constraining state action.[16] Their views of actor identities and preferences as fixed prevent them from considering how social interaction might produce cooperative norms and in turn changes in actor identities or the opposite, a faltering cooperative arrangement. Again, the notion and understanding of change is what social constructivists provide students of world politics; realism and liberalism lack this understanding.

Social constructivists look upon IOs like the EU as much more than a forum for facilitating cooperation among actors with static interests in maximizing economic gain. Constructivists are interested in the broader effects that organizations, as part of actors' social context, have. They are interested in how organizations shape not only how actors behave (i.e., liberals show how organizations can change cost/benefit calculations) but also how organizations shape what actors want (their interests) and who actors are (their identities).[17]

Constructivists would claim that if we want to understand European states' behavior, we must consider how the EU, a significant part of their social context, influences the interests and identities of those states. As just one example, in a discussion of the monetary union, Risse et al. claim that

> actors' perception of their material and instrumental interests with regard to the Euro are deeply influenced by their *visions* of European political order. Thus, the Euro is about European union and political order rather than only lowering transaction costs or creating exchange-rate stability.[18]

The states of the EU have ideas of "Europe"—what it is and what it signifies—that come to govern their interactions with one another and the political order in Europe. Thus, for social constructivists, the EU is not merely a forum to help states reach cooperative results. Instead, the EU is a fundamental part of the European states' social context. It is a forum that contains ideas, meanings, and rules that come to shape how these states view the world, how they view themselves, how they decide what they want, and how they decide to take action.[19]

Putting It All Together II: Human Rights and Security[20]

One hundred years ago, systems of apartheid could be found on almost every continent of the globe. Though the institution of slavery had lost legitimacy, the segregation of peoples based on physical characteristics, religion, tribe, or other group membership remained a common practice. In the United States, for example, the formal institution of slavery ended with the American Civil War but was quickly replaced by a system of legalized racial segregation, a system of "Jim Crow" laws and practices that denied African Americans equal access to resources, equal opportunity, and equal protection. Not until the 1960s was this system—sometimes referred to as "the American apartheid"[21]—finally deemed unconstitutional.

Of course, when most of us think of apartheid today, we think of South Africa, which formally ended its apartheid system in 1991. As Audie Klotz explains, in the mid-1980s, important changes took place in how the world viewed and responded to the South African apartheid. These changes, especially in U.S. policy, offer a good example of how a special class of ideas (in this case, global norms of racial equality) do not simply constrain behavior but can also redefine states' interests.

A hundred years ago, South Africa was the object of struggle between British colonizers and previous Dutch settlers. Though British colonizers did implement laws calling for the better treatment of nonwhites in South Africa, racial equality was far from a widely held norm. In fact, British ordinances on the subject were an important source of tension between the British and Dutch settlers. Even in the 1960s, when the formal system of apartheid—the "Grand Apartheid"—was adopted, few in the world (including the United States) took an active interest in, let alone opposition to, what is widely considered today an inhumane and unjust system.

Beyond National Interests: The Role of Social Norms

Traditional approaches offer a compelling explanation of U.S. policies until the mid-1980s. They argue that major powers did not see it in their material (strategic or economic) interests to force the white minority government to change its policies. For example, in the early 1980s, the United States claimed that Cold War strategic and economic interests, the need for continued access to South Africa's large mineral deposits, and concerns about vulnerable sea-lanes far outweighed U.S. interest in racial equality. U.S. inaction was also justified by ideas of sovereignty that deemed the internal affairs of states as off-limits to outside intervention. However, traditional approaches are less able to explain the U.S. decision to impose sanctions on the South African government in 1985–1986. Why did the United States decide to override ideas of sovereignty and impose sanctions on South Africa in the mid-1980s when there was no corresponding change in its economic and strategic situation? In fact, the Reagan administration at the time argued that U.S. strategic interests in South Africa had increased, not decreased. Why did the United States and the international community become concerned with the internal politics of South Africa? Traditional approaches are unable to explain the change.

Social constructivists argue that we have to pay attention to how norms can define states' interests. Norms are ideas that express "shared (social) understandings of standards for behavior."[22] In this case, a global norm of racial equality redefined how the United States understood its interests in South Africa. This norm did not have an automatic effect, however. UN resolutions supported a norm of racial equality as early as 1960, but the United States continued to veto any attempts to impose mandatory sanctions on the South African government. Klotz demonstrates how grassroots and transnational actors advocated for an anti-apartheid norm—raising public awareness about and mobilizing protests around the issue of apartheid. They did this by explicitly connecting the domestic conversation on civil rights in the United States to the international discussion on apartheid. This linkage was critical because it made it increasingly difficult for U.S. policy makers and corporations to continue doing business with South Africa without opening themselves up to charges of racism at home.

These activities made it clear that the social context within which the United States existed had changed and apartheid was seen as illegitimate. Faced with pressure from these groups throughout the 1980s, the anti-apartheid norm served to alter U.S. notions of its interests. Starting in Congress and eventually throughout the U.S. government, the United States now saw its interests tied to the promotion of racial equality in South Africa, resulting in the sanctioning of the South African government in 1985–1986. Such sanctions from the world's largest economic power and world community imposed important economic constraints on the South African government. These constraints, along with significant internal pressure and shrinking strategic leverage vis-à-vis the United States and the Soviet Union due to the ending of the Cold War, helped convince the South African government to formally end its system of apartheid in 1991.

The South African case illustrates a number of important constructivist points that contrast with those of dominant theories. First, norms matter. They do not necessarily determine outcomes, but they do help define and limit a range of acceptable policy choices and reformulate understandings of interest. In the case of South Africa, one could choose any number of ways to bring pressure on the South African government, but what was no longer okay was *not to do anything at all*. The global norm of racial equality had put tolerance for apartheid outside the range of legitimate U.S. options. Second, states are not the only actors that matter. Apartheid in South Africa was ended largely through the efforts of sub-state actors and a transnational coalition of actors and groups. Finally, change does not necessarily depend on leadership by powerful actors. In this case, the United States was a follower, not a leader, and transnational groups and weak states had an influence on U.S. policy far greater than their material resources and capabilities would suggest.

Putting It All Together III:
Traditional Security Considerations[23]

During the twentieth century, states developed a tremendous capacity to make war, but this has not meant that they are completely free to make use of the weapons available. The international community considers the use of some weapons, as in the case of chemical weapons, "taboo," even "unthinkable," in most situations.

Richard Price argues that the case of modern chemical weapons is unique because from the beginning, there was a sense in the international community that this category of weapon was contrary to the practices and ideals of a civilized society. In fact, as early as 1898, the Hague Declaration identified a ban on using such weapons in war. While this ban did not prevent combatants in World War I from using chemical weapons, it was an important factor in the prohibitions against their use in World War II. Today, chemical weapons are considered a particularly reprehensible category of weapon. They are especially not to be used against civilians. In cases where that expectation has been violated, it has been cause for international censure and calls for action. This includes contemporary cases like the Syrian civil war, where Russian interests have blocked UNSC action against Bashar al-Assad regime. Over one hundred countries in at least five United Nations General Assembly resolutions through 2016 "strongly condemn[ed]," "express[ed] outrage" and "grave concern" at the use of chemical weapons against civilians and "demand[ed]" that Syrian principals and authorities "strictly observe their obligations under international law with respect to chemical and biological weapons."[24] And even Russia in the UNSC condemned the use of toxic chemicals against civilians and supported the creation of a joint investigative mechanism into the matter.[25]

Beyond Material Power: Constructing Identity

What explains the general reluctance of states to use chemical weapons? Price asks, "How is it that among the countless technological innovations in weaponry that have been used by humankind, chemical weapons almost alone have come to be stigmatized as morally illegitimate?"[26] This confuses realists.[27] Why would states give up any tool for securing power? Standard arguments explain the general lack of use of chemical weapons by arguing that they are crueler or less useful than other weapons. However, it is difficult to conceive that death by asphyxiation is any worse than other means of dying or killing one another. In addition, these weapons have military utility. Their wide usage during World War I took place precisely because they were viewed as tactically valuable. Similarly, in debates about their regulation following World War I, military negotiators tried to prevent a comprehensive ban based on their perceived utility. The fact is that in any number of situations since World War I chemical weapons would have been useful and in the case of World War II, possibly decisive, yet with a few very notable exceptions, combatants did not use them because the participants recognized that this was a line they could not cross. Given their utility, realists have a difficult time understanding why states would limit themselves by banning these weapons.

Social constructivists focus on the social and cultural meanings and significance that society attaches to certain things and practices and thus they approach the chemical weapons ban differently. For constructivists, the taboo associated with the use of chemical weapons illustrates how certain ideas about ourselves—our identity—guide our behavior, even in warfare where physical survival is at stake. In this case, the nonuse of chemical weapons has stood as an important "marker of civilization." As such, the taboo against chemical weapons stems from our ideas about what constitutes a "civilized society" and what makes us "civilized people." This association between the nonuse of chemical weapons and a civilized society began with the Hague Declaration and continues to the present day. Think, for example, about recent discussions about chemical weapons: only individuals as "uncivilized" and "barbaric" as Saddam Hussein, Osama bin Laden, or Bashar al-Assad would think of using such weapons. In Saddam Hussein's case, his "barbarism" was confirmed twice over when the world learned of his gassing of Kurdish civilians in Iraq. And in the case of Bashar al-Assad, President Trump considered a 2017 chemical weapons attack so reprehensible that he responded with U.S. airstrikes.

By the same token, ideas of civilization have not protected all peoples equally. While the social and cultural meanings and significance society has attached to these weapons have acted as an important constraint on action, they have done so mainly against those whom actors have identified as civilized as they are. In other words, the rules and norms of warfare among "civilized" peoples/states are often understood as different from those governing warfare with or involving "uncivilized" peoples/states. For instance, Germany resisted using chemical weapons during the Allied invasion of Normandy in World War II, but arguably, the United States had less of a problem using a form of chemical weapons (napalm) in its war against Vietnam.

In short, constructivists concentrate on questions of interpretation and identity, on how states have understood these weapons and themselves, and how those ideas are translated into practice. The unique moral stigma associated with chemical weapons has far less to do with their inherent characteristics (e.g., their utility or inhumanity) and far more to do with "how civilizations and societies have interpreted those characteristics and translated them into practice."[28] Again, they are no less useful and no less humane than many other weapons, but states have identified these particular weapons as especially awful. States do not use them because that is not what civilized people do. Thus, writes Price, "abiding by or violating social norms is an important way by which we gauge 'who we are'—to be a certain kind of people means we just do not do certain things."[29]

Price's discussion of the chemical weapons ban also illustrates another constructivist insight, namely that norms, identities, and practices are mutually reinforcing but at the same time are subject to change. For example, the moral stigma associated with chemical weapons, according to Price, was a necessary but not sufficient factor in prohibiting their use since World War I. The stigma is what distinguishes chemical weapons from other weapons but had we allowed previous violations of the Hague declaration to go unchallenged—had their use in World War I not provoked the vigorous debate about their use and significance—chemical weapons might today be a perfectly acceptable form of warfare. This also underscores the constructivist point that positive behaviors, like a ban on chemical weapons, require reinforcement because actors' behaviors create expectations about what is appropriate behavior.

The perceived odiousness of chemical weapons has very much constrained actor behavior in ways unanticipated by other theories. Thus, the saying "All's fair in love and war" is not completely accurate because in the conduct of war, there are some practices and some weapons that are considered "not fair" and thus prohibited by international society. What is all the more amazing is that today, states not only take it as fact that such weapons are horrifying, but it is also no longer socially acceptable to openly question or debate whether they are in fact inhumane and immoral. They just are. The chemical weapons ban illustrates how certain ideas and practices build upon and reinforce one another to "produce and legitimate certain behaviors and conditions of life as 'normal.'"[30] In other words, some ideas and some practices become so established that we come to consider them simply "facts of life." This does not mean that those ideas and practices will not be open to reinterpretation or change at a later date; in fact, it is quite the contrary. By highlighting the process of social interpretation and reinterpretation, constructivism offers an approach to world politics that considers the important dynamism of political life. Some of the greatest—and often most subtle—changes stem from evolving ideas about *how* world politics should be conducted and relatedly how states and other actors think of themselves as members of particular world communities.

Lessons Learned: The Power of Ideas

These three examples have shown the power of ideas and given legitimacy to the constructivist argument that ideas and norms are a crucial factor in explaining world politics. Beginning with the dual notions that agents create their own contexts and the contexts shape agents, along with an emphasis on meanings, ideas, and norms, constructivists are able to explain change in world politics. They can show how states can escape the realist logic of anarchy—as the European states altered their behavior, they created a context of peace and security, where there once was war and suspicion. They can show how IOs are more than facilitators of mutual interests—the EU has come to fundamentally shape what European states want and who the European states consider themselves to be. They can show how U.S. policy toward the South African apartheid changed—through the actions of actors in world politics, an anti-apartheid norm arose and replaced the understanding that apartheid is an acceptable manner of organizing a society. They can show how chemical weapons became taboo—as states came to conceive of chemical weapons as barbaric, their actions reinforced the notion that any state that wants to consider itself or to be considered "civilized" will reject the use of chemical weapons.

In each case, the cycle of actors' behaviors and interactions created a new social context, and that context shaped those actors, giving rise to new ways of conceiving the world and relations between actors. It is the idea that European states are a peaceful community, the idea of a European identity, the idea that apartheid is unacceptable, and the idea that chemical weapons are taboo that shapes expectations and relations. Constructivists claim that ideas (norms, rules, meanings) are powerful and must be taken into account when explaining world politics—and the empirical cases they draw upon demonstrate that their claims are plausible.

However, though constructivists focus on the power of ideas, they do not ignore other sources of power. Material power is not irrelevant in constructivist analysis. It should be no surprise that not all ideas are equally significant. It makes a difference who is advocating what ideas. In the case of the EU, it is not coincidental that the United States supported and encouraged (if not demanded) the cooperative relations that altered anarchy in Europe. Similarly, the anti-apartheid movement was moving relatively slowly until it was able to change how the United States viewed the issue in South Africa. Once the United States was on board, the anti-apartheid norm quickly became more powerful and more easily replaced the norm that held that apartheid was acceptable. Finally, the great powers acted as the arbiters of civilization, deciding that chemical weapons were uncivilized. These great powers had (and continue to have) the power to make sure that others did not use chemical weapons and this added to the power of the chemical weapons taboo.

Does this mean that it is really just material power that matters? No. In all three of those cases, though the material power of large states was integral to the change that occurred, the material power itself tells us nothing about which direction change will go. The power of the United States and other great powers do not determine how they will act; even powerful states are shaped by their context. Recall the apartheid case. U.S. behavior itself was shaped by the international context that held that apartheid was unacceptable. In addition, though the United States may have helped to initiate cooperation in Europe, it was the actions and interactions of the European states that forged the zone of peace— the power of the United States may have gotten things started, but the outcome was more a result of the cycle of actors creating their context and the context shaping the actors. In constructivist analysis, then, ideas play a central role, but it is the interaction of material power and the power of ideas that explain phenomena in world politics.

Finally, as a note of caution, constructivist tools do not work to explain only the happy phenomena in world politics. Objectionable phenomena are socially constructed too. While we have highlighted three positive changes in world politics—the growth of peace in Europe, the elimination of apartheid, and the taboo restricting the use of chemical weapons—we must remember that in each of those cases, the preceding conditions were socially constructed as well.

In the case of the EU, throughout most of the modern history of Europe, states behaved and interacted in ways that made anarchy just the way that realists conceive of it—as a condition that necessarily leads to suspicion, insecurity, and conflict. Some are predicting that with the rise of populist movements across Europe and the looming prospect of Brexit, this may once again be the norm. In the case of apartheid, there were international norms upholding the acceptability of apartheid— norms of sovereignty that forbid interference in another state and norms that restricted which groups of people qualify for human rights.[31] Finally, in the case of chemical weapons, the "civilized" great powers deemed them entirely usable in World War I, and the identity "civilized" was not constructed to include the nonuse of chemical weapons. Thus, just as ideas like universal human rights, peace, and democracy can come to define a social context and shape actors' identities, interests, and behaviors, so can ideas about oppression and conflict.

Indeed, we may be witnessing and participating in an instance of socially constructed conflict in the world around us today. In a famous (or infamous depending on your opinion) article, Samuel Huntington described what he calls the "Clash of Civilizations." He hypothesizes that the nature of conflict has changed over time—from conflict between princes (early history through seventeenth century) to conflict between nations (eighteenth and nineteenth centuries) to conflict between ideologies (twentieth century) and now to conflict between civilizations. He views civilizations as the highest and broadest groupings of human beings and that potential conflict will arise on the "fault lines" between civilizations.[32]

This is a perfect example of the social construction of conflict. Huntington notes several "objective" characteristics that civilizations share, but even Huntington admits that "subjective self-identification" is necessary for a civilization to exist as a distinct group. Remember that a social context—like a notion of an overarching civilization—requires that actors act in a way that produces that context. In order for a civilization to be a meaningful concept, actors have to believe they are a part of the civilization and act in ways that make the civilization real. The notion of a civilization is a socially constructed idea. In addition, even if Huntington is right that civilizations have objective elements (elements that are real regardless of what actors do or say), the notion of civilizational conflict is certainly constructed. As we learned in the case of the EU, actors create their own context—there is no inevitability to conflict between actors (civilizations or otherwise) unless actors' actions and interactions create a conflictual social context.

The idea of civilizational conflict is a powerful one, and one that has the potential to construct world affairs in a dangerous manner. Consider the rhetoric surrounding the September 11 attacks and the U.S. response to them. There are a number of people who discuss this tragedy and its aftermath in terms of the West versus Islam.[33] And with subsequent extremist attacks in Berlin, Paris, and numerous other cities around the world, this narrative continues to grow and reinforces the social construction of civilizational conflict. Indeed, as one observer has noted,

> Moreover, if we treat all states who are part of some other "civilization" as intrinsically hostile, we are likely to create enemies that might otherwise be neutral or friendly. In fact, a civilizational approach to foreign policy is probably the surest way to get diverse foreign cultures to coordinate their actions and could even bring several civilizations together against us . . . . In this sense, The Clash of Civilizations offers a dangerous, self-fulfilling prophecy: The more we believe it and make it the basis for action, the more likely it is to come true. Huntington would no doubt feel vindicated, but the rest of us would not be happy with the results.[34]

Wrap-Up

Here is the take-home message. Constructivism is an approach to world politics that facilitates explaining change in a dynamic international system. It can do this because it focuses on three things.

- The power of ideas in defining ranges of action in world politics.
- The importance of identity in defining what actors want.
- The importance of the cyclical relationship between actors' interests, identities, and behavior and the social context in which they exist.

Taken together, these insights help us to understand how the world and world politics is constructed for both good and ill.

Further Reading

1. Jeffrey Checkel, "The Constructivist Turn in International Relations Theory" (1998), examines three important constructivist books. He lays out well the tenets of constructivism and highlighting both the advantages and disadvantages of constructivist analysis.
2. Martha Finnemore, *National Interests in International Society* (1996), is a sophisticated, yet clearly written constructivist volume. She provides a good introduction to constructivism and three case studies that examine how IOs teach states to behave (UNESCO and science policy; Red Cross and conduct in war; the World Bank and development policy).
3. Ronnie Lipshutz, "Because People Matter: Studying Global Political Economy" (2001), does a good job locating constructivism and other critical theories in relation to mainstream IR theory. In addition, it is a notable article making a case for why theoretical perspective matters in how we approach the global political economy.
4. Nicholas Onuf, "Constructivism: A User's Manual" (1998), is a very suitable introduction to constructivism for students that have had some exposure to IR theory. It can work in introductory classes as well if the students are introduced to constructivism first.
5. Karen Fierke and Knud Jorgensen, *Constructing International Relations: The Next Generation* (2001), brings together a distinguished set of authors to discuss various aspects and nuances of constructivism. The volume nicely lays out the various strains of constructivist thought and provides a good introduction to using constructivism.
6. Emanuel Adler, "Seizing the Middle Ground" (1997), is an in-depth treatment of constructivist theory. It is especially useful for tracing out the different strains of constructivist thought and placing constructivism in relation to other approaches to world politics.
7. John Ruggie, *Constructing the World Polity: Essays on International Institutionalization*, especially the chapter, "What Makes the World Hang Together: Neo-Utilitarianism and the Social Constructivist

Challenge" (1998), contains a very sophisticated treatment of constructivism that advanced students will appreciate, but that may confuse undergraduates with less experience exploring IR theory.

8. Alexander Wendt, "The Agent-Structure Problem in International Relations" (1992), was one of the first social constructivist treatments in IR. It is a dense article, but in it, Wendt traces out the theoretical and philosophical basis for social constructivist thought. Advanced students will enjoy going to the source after being introduced to constructivism and reading other works by Wendt.

9. Friedrich Kratochwil, *Rules, Norms, and Decisions* (1989), provides a sophisticated analysis of how aspects of actors' social context— rules and norms—emerge and come to influence actors in IR.

Notes

An earlier version of this chapter appeared as "Making and Remaking the World for IR 101: A Resource for Teaching Social Constructivism in Introductory Classes." *International Studies Review* (2003) v. 4:1, 15–33.

[1] Our choice to juxtapose social constructivism against realism and liberalism is mirrored in significant works in the literature (see, e.g., John Ruggie, *Constructing the World Polity: Essays on International Institutionalization* [London: Routledge, 1998] and Alexander Wendt, *Social Theory of International Politics* [Cambridge: Cambridge University Press, 1999]) that contrasts social constructivism with "rationalist" approaches to international relations. Further, our discussion of realism and liberalism is restricted to their dominant strains: neorealism and neoliberal institutionalism. We are aware that different versions of realism and liberalism may have different areas of agreement and disagreement with constructivism, but for the sake of clarity, we have chosen to restrict our discussion to neorealism and neoliberalism. Throughout the chapter, we therefore use neorealism/ neoliberalism interchangeably with realism/liberalism.

[2] The apartheid and chemical weapons cases lend themselves well to working with a single, seminal work—Audie Klotz (1995) for apartheid, and Richard Price (1997) for the chemical weapons ban. Because the EU is a more complex case with no single, definitive treatment, we draw on numerous sources to demonstrate a constructivist account.

[3] If students would like to learn more about the lineage and foundations of realism, see, e.g., Thucydides, *The Peloponnesian War* (Suffolk, England: Penguin Books, 1975); E. H. Carr, *The Twenty Years' Crisis, 1919–1939*, 2nd edition (New York: Harper and Row, 1964); Hans Morgenthau, *Politics among Nations: The Struggle for Power and Peace*, 3rd edition (New York: Alfred A. Knopf, 1962); and Kenneth N. Waltz, *Theory of International Politics* (New York: McGraw-Hill, 1979).

[4] If students would like to learn more about the lineage and foundations of liberalism, see, e.g., Immanuel Kant, *Perpetual Peace: A Philosophical Essay* (New York: Garland, 1972); Robert Keohane, *After Hegemony: Cooperation and Discord in the World Political Economy* (Princeton, NJ: Princeton University Press, 1984); and Michael W. Doyle, *Ways of War and Peace: Realism, Liberalism, and Socialism* (New York: W.W. Norton, 1997).

5 If students would like to learn more about the lineage and foundations of constructivism, see, e.g., Max Weber, *The Theory of Social and Economic Organization* (New York: The Free Press, 1964); Anthony Giddens, *The Constitution of Society* (Berkeley: University of California Press, 1984); and Wendt, *Social Theory of International Politics*.

6 For an interesting article that explains how ideas can shape the boundaries of possible behavior, see Albert S. Yee, "The Causal Effect of Ideas on Policies," *International Organization* 50, no. 1 (1996): 69–108.

7 If students are interested in going further on sovereignty, see, e.g., Samuel J. Barkin and Bruce Cronin, "The State and the Nation: Changing Norms and the Rules of Sovereignty in International Relations," *International Organization* 48, no. 1 (1994): 107–30; Robert H. Jackson, *Quasi-States: Sovereignty, International Relations and the Third World* (Cambridge: Cambridge University Press, 1990); and Stephen D. Krasner, "Sovereignty: An Institutional Perspective," *Comparative Political Studies* 21 (1988): 66–94.

8 The following case discussions are designed to give a broad sense of what constructivists argue; they are not definitive explanations, nor are they tests of constructivist hypotheses.

9 Alexander Wendt, "Anarchy is What States Make of It: The Social Construction of Power Politics," *International Organization* 46, no. 2 (1992): 391–425.

10 Richard N. Lebow, "The Long Peace, the End of the Cold War, and the Failure of Realism," *International Organization* 48, no. 2 (1994): 251.

11 At least one realist observer thought that this was likely. See Mearsheimer (1990).

12 Adler 1997a: 276.

13 Lebow, "The Long Peace, the End of the Cold War, and the Failure of Realism," 269.

14 Especially when a dominant power like the United States is providing a good deal of the external security for these nations.

15 Katzenstein, Peter J. 1996. "Introduction." In *The Culture of National Security*, P. Katzenstein, ed. (New York: Columbia University Press, 1996), 13.

16 Alastair I. Johnston, "Treating International Institutions as Social Environments," *International Studies Quarterly* 45, no. 4 (2001): 487.

17 Mark A. Pollack, "International Relations Theory and European Integration," *Journal of Common Market Studies* 39, no. 2 (2001): 234–37.

18 Thomas Risse et al., "To Euro or Not to Euro? The EMU and Identity Politics in the European Union," *European Journal of International Relations* 5, no. 2 (1999): 148, emphasis added.

19 If students would like to go further on the EU, see, e.g., Andrew Moravcsik, *The Choice for Europe: Social Purpose and State Power from Messina to Maastricht* (Ithaca, NY: Cornell University Press, 1998); Symposium on the European Union, *Journal of European Public Policy* 6, no. 4 (1999).

20 The argument and case description in this section draws primarily from Klotz, 1995.

21 Douglas S. Massey and Nancy A. Denton, *American Apartheid: Segregation and the Making of the Underclass* (Cambridge, MA: Harvard University Press, 1993).

22 Audie Klotz, "Norms Reconstituting Interests: Global Racial Equality and U.S. Sanctions against South Africa," *International Organization* 49, no. 3 (1995): 451.

[23] The argument and case description in this section draws primarily from Price 1995 and 1997.

[24] See UNGA resolutions: A/RES/66/253 B (August 3, 2012); A/RES/67/262 (May 15, 2013); A/RES/68/182 (December 18, 2013); A/RES/71/130 (December 9, 2016); A/RES/71/248 (December 21, 2016).

[25] See UNSC resolutions: S/RES/2209 (March 6, 2015); S/RES/2235 (August 7, 2015); S/RES/2314 (October 31, 2016; S/RES/2319 (November 17, 2016), all of which Russia voted affirmatively.

[26] Richard Price, "A Genealogy of the Chemical Weapons Taboo," *International Organization* 49, no. 1 (1995): 73.

[27] Neoliberal analysis is more appropriate for economic issues, and neoliberals tend to avoid security issues like the chemical weapons ban. Thus, in this section, we contrast the social constructivist explanation with the realist argument alone.

[28] Richard Price, *The Chemical Weapons Taboo* (Ithaca, NY: Cornell University Press, 1997), 6.

[29] Price, *The Chemical Weapons Taboo*, 10.

[30] Price, "A Genealogy of the Chemical Weapons Taboo," 87.

[31] Klotz, "Norms Reconstituting Interests"; Martha Finnemore, "Constructing Norms of Humanitarian Intervention," in *The Culture of National Security*, P. Katzenstein, ed. (New York: Columbia University Press, 1996a), 153–85.

[32] Samuel P. Huntington, "The Clash of Civilizations?" *Foreign Affairs* 72, no. 3 (1993): 24–29.

[33] Huntington did not focus on the West-Islam conflict to the neglect of other potential conflicts. He argued that conflict would come at the fault lines between eight major civilizations (West, Islam, Confucian [China for the most part], Japanese, Hindu, Slavic-Orthodox, Latin American, African).

[34] Stephen M. Walt, "The Clash of Civilizations and the Remaking of World Order," *Foreign Policy*, no. 106 (1997): 189.

Works Cited

Adler, Emanuel. 1997a. "Imagined (Security) Communities: Cognitive Regions in International Relations." *Millennium: Journal of International Studies.* 26, no. 2: 249–77.

Adler, Emanuel. 1997b. "Seizing the Middle Ground: Constructivism in World Politics." *European Journal of International Relations.* 3: 319–63.

Barkin, Samuel J., and Bruce Cronin. 1994. "The State and the Nation: Changing Norms and the Rules of Sovereignty in International Relations." *International Organization.* 48, no. 1: 107–30.

Carr, E. H. 1964. *The Twenty Years' Crisis, 1919–1939*, 2nd edition. New York: Harper and Row.

Checkel, Jeffrey. 1998. "The Constructivist Turn in International Relations Theory." *World Politics.* 50, no. 2: 324–48.

Doyle, Michael W. 1997. *Ways of War and Peace: Realism, Liberalism, and Socialism.* New York: W.W. Norton.

Fierke, Karen M., and Knud Erik Jørgensen, eds. 2001. *Constructing International Relations: The Next gGeneration.* Armonk, NY: M.E. Sharpe.

Finnemore, Martha. 1996a. "Constructing Norms of Humanitarian Intervention." In P. Katzenstein, ed. *The Culture of National Security*, 153–85. New York: Columbia University Press.

Finnemore, Martha. 1996b. *National Interests in International Society*. Ithaca, NY: Cornell University Press.

Giddens, Anthony. 1984. *The Constitution of Society*. Berkeley: University of California Press.

Huntington, Samuel P. 1993. "The Clash of Civilizations?" *Foreign Affairs*. 72, no. 3: 22–49.

Jackson, Robert H. 1990. *Quasi-States: Sovereignty, International Relations and the Third World*. Cambridge: Cambridge University Press.

Johnston, Alastair I. 2001. "Treating International Institutions as Social Environments." *International Studies Quarterly*. 45, no. 4: 487–515.

Kant, Immanuel. 1972. *Perpetual Peace: A Philosophical Essay*. New York: Garland.

Keohane, Robert. 1984. *After Hegemony: Cooperation and Discord in the World Political Economy*. Princeton, NJ: Princeton University Press.

Katzenstein, Peter J. 1996. "Introduction." In P. Katzenstein, ed. *The Culture of National Security*, 1–32. New York: Columbia University Press.

Klotz, Audie. 1995. "Norms Reconstituting Interests: Global Racial Equality and U.S. Sanctions Against South Africa." *International Organization*. 49, no. 3: 451–78.

Krasner, Stephen D. 1988. "Sovereignty: An Institutional Perspective." *Comparative Political Studies*. 21: 66–94.

Kratochwil, Friedrich. 1989. *Rules, Norms, and Decisions: On the Conditions of Practical and Legal Reasoning in International Relations and Domestic Affairs*. Cambridge: Cambridge University Press.

Lebow, Richard N. 1994. "The Long Peace, the End of the Cold War, and the Failure of Realism." *International Organization*. 48, no. 2: 249–77.

Lipshutz, Ronnie D. 2001. "Because People Matter: Studying Global Political Economy." *International Studies Perspectives*. 2, no. 4: 321–39.

Massey, Douglas S., and Nancy A. Denton. 1993. *American Apartheid: Segregation and the Making of the Underclass*. Cambridge, MA: Harvard University Press.

Mearsheimer, John J. 1990. "Back to the Future: Instability in Europe after the Cold War." *International Security*. 15: 5–56.

Moravcsik, Andrew. 1998. *The Choice for Europe: Social Purpose and State Power from Messina to Maastricht*. Ithaca, NY: Cornell University Press.

Morgenthau, Hans. 1962. *Politics among Nations: The Struggle for Power and Peace*, 3rd edition. New York: Alfred A. Knopf.

Onuf, Nicholas. 1998. "Constructivism: A User's Manual." In V. Kubalkova, N. Onuf, and P. Kowert, eds. *International Relations in a Constructed World*, 58–78. Armonk, NY: M.E. Sharpe.

Pollack, Mark A. 2001. "International Relations Theory and European Integration." *Journal of Common Market Studies*. 39, no. 2: 221–44.

Price, Richard. 1997. *The Chemical Weapons Taboo*. Ithaca, NY: Cornell University Press.

Price, Richard. 1995. "A Genealogy of the Chemical Weapons Taboo." *International Organization*. 49, no. 1: 73–103.

Risse, Thomas, Daniela Engelmann-Martin, Hans-Joachim Knope and Klaus Roscher. 1999. "To Euro or Not to Euro? The EMU and Identity Politics in the European Union." *European Journal of International Relations.* 5, no. 2: 147–87.

Ruggie, John. 1998. *Constructing the World Polity: Essays on International Institutionalization.* London: Routledge.

Symposium on the European Union. 1999. *Journal of European Public Policy.* 6, no. 4.

Thucydides. 1975. *The Peloponnesian War.* Suffolk, England: Penguin Books.

Walt, Stephen M. 1997. "The Clash of Civilizations and the Remaking of World Order." *Foreign Policy,* no. 106: 176–89.

Waltz, Kenneth N. 1979. *Theory of International Politics.* New York: McGraw-Hill.

Weber, Max. 1964. *The Theory of Social and Economic Organization.* New York: The Free Press.

Wendt, Alexander. 1987. "The Agent-Structure Problem in International Relations Theory." *International Organization.* 41, no. 3: 335–70.

Wendt, Alexander. 1992. "Anarchy is What States Make of It: The Social Construction of Power Politics." *International Organization.* 46, no. 2: 391–425.

Wendt, Alexander. 1999. *Social Theory of International Politics.* Cambridge: Cambridge University Press.

Yee, Albert S. 1996. "The Causal Effect of Ideas on Policies." *International Organization.* 50, no. 1: 69–108.

CHAPTER 6

Feminism
Seeing Gender in Global Politics

Laura Sjoberg

Have you ever thought about what it would be like if women ran the world? Asking yourself that question might tell you a lot about not only what you think about yourself but also what you think about global politics, and what you think about gender.

Would the world be more peaceful if women ran it? Or, as Robin Williams once joked at the Met in a stand-up comedy routine, would "there be no more war, but stern negotiations every 28 days?" Would there be more care? Or more backstabbing? Or would the world be no different?

Would it make a difference if women were integrated into world leadership "naturally" at the current rate (where world governments would become gender-equal around the year 2500) or if the current gender makeup of world leadership (which is about 80 percent male in executive and legislative branches) was reversed tomorrow?

If you think the world would be different if women ran it, why? Is it because men and women are naturally different sorts of people? Or because boys play with trucks and girls play with dolls? Or because of some other social conditioning?

Also, there are not more men in the world than there are women. So, if women are underrepresented in the halls of power in global politics, where are they overrepresented? If, as the statistics say, all across the world, women are overrepresented in poverty, as single parents, and in low-paying jobs, is that just a coincidence? Or is it a result of gender discrimination and subordination?

These are the sort of questions that feminist theorizing in IR asks about the world around us. Feminist theorizing is not about affirmative action or arguing that women are better than men. Instead, it is about exploring the role that gender plays in global politics, from individual people's lives to state interaction.

This chapter begins with a discussion of the meaning of gender and moves to discussing the study of gender, generally and in the discipline of IR specifically. It then explores the contribution of feminist work to the study of global politics, as both a whole field of "feminist IR" and then as different feminisms uniquely. After laying that groundwork, the chapter briefly discusses feminist contributions to two major areas in IR: security and political economy.

Thinking Like a Feminist

What are the places in your life that you might be treated differently because you are identified as a man or as a woman? What advantages and disadvantages does that identification get you in a classroom? In a workplace? In a shopping mall? In a car dealership? In your personal relationships? Are you insulted when (if you identify as a man) you are called effeminate? Or (if you identify as a woman) you are called masculine or manly? Why or why not? What power do these labels have in our daily lives?

There are some places in global politics it is easy to see gender oppression, like in the households, sweatshops, and camp towns that feminist political economists see. But it is often just as easy to say that it is sad that women around the world are unequal, but women "here" are fortunate enough not to have those problems. In other words, many people are feminists looking outside their own lives, but cannot see the gender subordination right here. If you looked through those lenses at "our" lives critically, where might you see that gender matters, not just in global politics but also in daily life? You might see it in income inequality at work, or the continued prevalence of sexual and domestic violence against women, or in gender-based expectations of political candidates, or even in this classroom.

What Is Gender?

Most of us have an understanding of what gender is, whether we have ever really thought about it or not. After all, we are asked about it on our tax forms and on applications for drivers' licenses, insurance, loans, and jobs. Some forms that we have to fill out ask what our "sex" is, while others ask what our "gender" is, but both give us two choices: male and female. We know, and have known since before we could remember, what it means to be a part of each of those categories, right? "Males" have sex organs associated with maleness (particularly, penises), and "females" have sex organs associated with femaleness (particularly vaginas), a difference that can be traced to XX and XY chromosomal combinations.

The words "sex" and "gender" are not always used as synonyms. Usually, the word "sex" is used to indicate membership in a biological category understood as male or female, while "gender" is used to talk about the social characteristics associated with biological sex. Even biological sex, however, is not as simple as the forms make it seem. In fact, fully 1 percent of the human population does not fit neatly into one of the two well-known biological sex categories. Many physical and genetic combinations are classified as "intersex," where someone has some attributes associated with maleness and some associated with femaleness. Until recently, most of these people's sex was "decided" as male or female at birth, but the medical community has become more aware of the existence of sex categories outside of male and female.

Even though biological sex is more complicated than the dichotomy between male and female, society often encourages us not only to identify with a sex but also to "act like" people in our sex category should. This is where the term "gender" comes into the conversation. "Gender" is the social expectations assigned to people based on their assumed membership in sex categories. Men are expected to be masculine, while women are expected to be feminine.

When a high school football coach tells a quarterback that he "throws like a girl," or a clique calls a girl a "tomboy," they are referring to an expected set of characteristics associated with that person's (presumed) biological sex, and accusing the person of not living up to those social expectations. Characteristics associated with masculinity include strength, rationality, autonomy, aggressiveness, independence, competition, materiality, bravery, and objectivity. Characteristics associated with femininity include weakness, emotion, interdependence, care, need for protection, compromise and negotiation, passiveness, and subjectivity. Men and masculinity are often associated with the public sphere and the business world, whereas women and femininity are often associated with the home and the private sphere.

Expectations about what it means to be a woman or what it means to be a man are everywhere in society—in the daily lives of "normal" people, on the cover of fashion and body-building magazines, and in campaigns for public office. Still, there is not just one idea of what it means to be masculine or what it means to be feminine. Instead, there are a number of competing masculinities and femininities. The masculinity expected by a football coach and the masculinity expected by a military commander have commonalities, but they also have differences. The "ideal" straight man is different from the "ideal" gay man—and those differ over time, place, and culture. Feminist scholars have identified the culturally dominant images of masculinity and femininity as "hegemonic," with other masculinities and femininities being subordinate to the hegemonic masculinity or femininity in the particular cultural and historical context.

"Gender," then, is what political scientists and social theorists have identified as a social construct—a product and a producer of human social expectations. Gender-based characteristics are things that we expect of people we understand to be men and women. We also assign gender-based characteristics to ideas, institutions, governments, and companies, among other things, around the world. For example, we often call the earth and the United States "mother earth" and the "motherland," whereas we assign masculine characteristics to other sociocultural phenomena, like "Father time." These gender-based dichotomies have, many times, served to organize thinking about social and political life.

The Study of Gender

The academic study of gender began in earnest in the 1960s, when scholars started to ask questions about why women were treated unequally in social, political, and economic life. People who studied gender from what is usually characterized as a "liberal" point of view argued that the problem was not with how the world was organized but instead with its exclusion of women from the halls of power. In other words, the "problem" of gender inequality could be fixed by giving women equal access to jobs, political positions, and education in the existing industries, government organizations, and school systems.

Another group of feminist scholars, however, identified themselves as "standpoint" feminists, arguing that there is something unique about women's experiences (not necessarily about women biologically, but about how women experience life in a gender-unequal society) that means that they have different (and valuable) perspectives on life, work, and politics. An example of such an argument in the recent media was during the confirmation hearings for now-Supreme Court Justice Sonia Sotomayer. Almost immediately after her nomination, newspapers quoted the Justice as having said eight years earlier that she "accept[s] that our experience of women and people of color affect our decisions" and arguing that the impact of her race and gender on her decision making was a mantle she carried proudly onto the bench. This statement would be an example of a standpoint feminist understanding.

A third group of feminist scholars, often characterized as "radical" feminists, argue that liberal feminists focus on integrating women into positions of power in society but ignore that those positions, their responsibilities, and their goals were all established when women were not represented in the halls of power. In other words, the "rules" of success in our social, political, and corporate worlds were made *by men for men*, so it would be silly, in "radical" feminists' view, for women to accept them as the right rules for everyone. "Radical" feminists argue that liberal feminism tries, in some sense, to put a square peg in a round hole, by integrating women into a world that remains dominated by masculinity even if not by men. Radical feminists argue that the gendered nature of the social, political, and economic structures of the world has to change in order to make ending gender subordination possible. They argue that the "rules" of our world need to be reevaluated and made gender-inclusive, rather than just encouraging women to follow men's examples.

While there are different approaches to feminism, each shares certain understandings of the world. You might have noticed that all three approaches to the study of gender I have listed have a political agenda. This in itself is a controversial move in the scholarly community. Many scholars adhere to some (sometimes more complicated) version of the scientific method in their understandings of how politics should be studied. These scholars argue that the study of politics is an objective science that can be pursued by asking research questions, forming hypotheses, testing those hypotheses with data, analyzing the results, and forming conclusions. Scholars who study gender, though, have a long history of questioning the possibility of separating knowledge from the perspective of the person who knows it. Instead, they have argued that all scholars study politics through particular "lenses"—prioritizing some things and setting aside others based on their worldviews and political priorities.

It is important to note, then, that feminist scholarship and the feminist political movement are not entirely separate. If *feminism* as a political movement is interested in making sure that the differences between men and women, whether natural or social, do not provide grounds for discrimination against women, then feminist scholarship is scholarship with a political interest in observing, understanding, and redressing that gender subordination. The study of gender, in sociology, law, and philosophy, like the study of gender in politics, has focused on not just looking at and studying the world objectively, but instead looking at and studying what is wrong with the world and how to fix it.

Studying Gender in International Relations

While the academic study of feminism took off in the 1960s with the globalization of the feminist movement, feminist work came into the discipline of IR a little bit later. There are those who, though generally receptive to the idea that women should be equal in the world, argue that the study of gender has no place in IR, considering that a substantial amount of IR scholarship addresses interstate relations and the international system. Many IR scholars admit that their work does not address gender issues, but argue that they are justified in failing to do so because their task is to study interstate relations and the international system *as they are* rather than as they should be. Those scholars, then, argue that their work, which ignores gender, simply replicates the "real world" of global politics, which does the same thing.[1]

In the late 1980s, feminist scholars entered the study of IR making two arguments against the contention that gender has no place in IR. The first argument they made is that women matter to global politics, whether or not they are in the places that global politics traditionally studies. They therefore asked the question, "Where are the women?" of global politics and IR. The second argument that they made was that women's exclusion from the positions of power and wealth in global life is not incidental, but structural—because the structures of global politics select for values and characteristics associated with masculinity. Feminists claimed that only by introducing gender analysis could the differential impact of the state system and the global economy on men and women's lives be understood.

It might be opportune here to situate the entry of feminist work into IR in the field more broadly. There are those who characterize the study of "International Relations" as a subfield of political science, and others who see it as an interdisciplinary effort. Both of those groups, however, generally told disciplinary history in the twentieth century as a series of "debates." The first debate, according to these scholars, was between realists (who saw the international arena as inherently conflictual) and idealists (who saw a potential to mitigate and possibly end conflict). The realists were said to have won this debate, and soon after, the second debate broke out—between those who insisted on a scientific approach to the study of global politics and those interested in a more historical or interpretive approach. Though the second debate remained settled on the side of the advocates of a scientific approach for quite a while, the end of the Cold War brought a time of change for the field of IR. The "third debate," then, began in the late 1980s and early 1990s, and has generally been characterized as a debate between "positivist" and "post-positivist" approaches.

In this third debate, some scholars began to question how the field saw the world, and how it measured knowledge. Post-positivist scholars argued that traditional (positivist) approaches were wrong in their understanding that universal, objective knowledge was a possible or desirable goal of the study of global politics.

While feminist theory has a fair amount in common with the "post-positivist" side of the third debate, they should not be seen as the same thing. Most feminists share the post-positivist commitment to examining the relationship between knowledge and power. While conventional IR often relies on explanations that ignore the social properties of the international arena, feminist theory (like most post-positivist work) focuses on social relations, particularly gender relations. Still, other "post-positivist" theories, like critical theory, postmodern theory, and even postcolonial theory, have often been as slow as traditional IR to introduce gender analysis into their work. As a result, feminist scholarship has been critical of both sides of the "third debate," and looked to explain gender as crucial to understanding global politics as a whole.

Gender and Global Politics

As I mentioned above, one of the early feminist questions about IR was a curiosity about where to find women in global politics. In *Bananas, Beaches, and Bases,* Cynthia Enloe used the Iran–Contra affair to look at the question of where women were in global politics. She argued that

> If we listened to women more carefully—to those trying to break out of the strait-jacket of conventional femininity *and* to those who find security and satisfaction in those very conventions— . . . we might find that the Iran/Contra affair and international politics generally looked different . . . . Making women invisible hides the workings of both femininity and masculinity in international politics.[2]

Feminists looking for women in global politics have found out a lot about where they are. Katharine Moon (1997) uncovered serious negotiations and a threatened withdrawal of U.S. troops in South Korea concerning the availability and STD testing of prostitutes in camp towns near bases. Christine Chin (1998) found women trafficked illegally as household workers and abused by employers in Malaysia as a symbol of modernity and middle-class status. Megan MacKenzie (2009) found women soldiers reticent to go through the Disarmament, Demobilization, and Reintegration (DDR) process in post-conflict Sierra Leone because of fear of stigma and lack of interest in returning to traditional family structures. Cynthia Enloe (1993) found women in exploited positions in the tourism industry, serving as symbols of exoticism, and (2004) as underpaid workers in sweatshop conditions in shoe factories. Elisabeth Prugl (1999) found women overrepresented among home-based workers, lobbying and playing complicated roles in the passage of the International Labor Organization's Homework Convention. Catia Confortini (2010) found women advocating for peace as a part of the Women's

International League for Peace and Freedom, while Caron Gentry and I (2007) found women as war criminals, terrorists, and perpetrators of genocide. Brooke Ackerly (2001) found women in India serving as each other's support systems to cope with rampant domestic violence in their rural communities. Jean Elshtain (1987) found women in wars even when they did not fight: as the stereotyped innocents and "beautiful souls" for whose protection wars are justified and fought. Joyce Kaufman and Kristen Williams (2007) found women's marriage habits to be an important element of nationalism in a number of case studies around the world, particularly in Northern Ireland. Heidi Hudson (2009) found women's movements negotiating the tense boundaries between feminist, nationalist, and peace-building goals in African post-conflict situations, struggling for inclusion in the political process while struggling to define their negotiation process. Denise Horn (2010) found women as military wives, providing the home services and motivation necessary for soldiers to fight wars. Francine D'Amico and Peter Beckman (1995) found some women as heads of state and in other positions of political, military, and economic power, battling stereotypes that assume women's inadequacy to the task of governing while trying to govern. Claudia Card (1996) found that women were the victims of systematic and often intentional wartime rape campaigns.

These studies are just the tip of the iceberg in terms of where feminists have looked to address the question "Where are the women?" in global politics. While there is no doubt that women's position (generally, and in most cases, specifically) has improved around the world, women are not yet equal to men. Around the world, poverty rates are substantially higher for women than for men, and this statistic crosses all national borders and the great majority of subgroups within all the nations in the world. Women in lesser-developed countries and minority women in developed countries are hit particularly hard by poverty. Women's overrepresentation among the world's poorest people is true whether or not they have children. Women's income, as relates to men's, has increased over the last fifty years, but in the best places in the world, women still earn less than 80 percent of what men do. This is partly because women remain segregated into low-paying occupations, and occupations dominated by women pay poorly. But it is also that overt discrimination continues to exist. For example, in the United States, full-time, year-round female workers with a bachelor's degree were paid 14 percent less than men in 2007.[3] Women are underrepresented in positions of power in the economy (they were only twelve of the Fortune 500 CEOs in 2009) and overrepresented in domestic work, unpaid labor, and human trafficking. The United Nations Development Fund for Women reports, "women represent 70 percent of the world's poor" with "the average wage gap in 2008 being 17 percent."[4]

Women are also underrepresented in the governance of every country in the world and have been so at every point in modern history. Women's representation in parliaments around the world is at a historic high: women constitute about 17 percent of the world's legislators. Women remain scarcely represented in cabinets and constitute less than 10 percent of the world's heads of state and government. In 2008, Rwandans elected the world's first (and only) woman-majority parliament. While 132 countries have populations that are majority women, only 17 have more than 30 percent women in their parliament (Rwanda, Sweden, South Africa, Spain, Norway, the Netherlands, New Zealand, Mozambique, Guyana, Germany, Finland, Denmark, Cuba, Costa Rica, Belgium, Austria, and Argentina). Several of those states are not classified as democracies by most international measures, and a number of them enforce gender quotas for their election of representatives.

Women remain more likely than not to face abuse from employers, partners, husbands, families, and community members, which is considered beyond the reach of domestic and international laws. Women continue to have less access to education, employment, housing, and health care than men in every state around the world. Women are more likely to die of starvation and preventable disease and have the highest rate of HIV/AIDS infection among groups around the world. Amnesty International reports that rape of Darfuri women in refugee camps remains "a daily occurrence" despite UN pretensions to supervision.[5] Gendered assumptions continue to pervade the security arena,[6] and women remain disproportionately negatively affected by many contemporary conflicts.[7]

These things remain true despite the fact that policy makers are increasingly talking about gender issues and doing so with increasing sophistication. In 2008, United Nations Security Council Resolution 1820 emphasized the importance of inviting women "to participate in discussions pertinent to the prevention and resolution of conflict, the maintenance of peace and security, and post-conflict peacebuilding" and encouraged "all parties to such talks to facilitate equal and full participation of women at all decision-making levels" *because* "women are key to international peace and security."[8] In 2009, the International Institute for Democracy and Electoral Assistance (IDEA) launched a "democracy and gender" campaign, insisting that women's political participation is key to the successful establishment and sustainability of democracy globally. The International Monetary Fund (IMF) is increasingly endorsing a concept called "gender budgeting," which "refers to the systematic examination of budget programs and policies for their impact on women" not only to promote gender equality but also to increase efficiency in budgeting.[9] The October 2009 focus campaign for Human Rights Watch was women's rights in India—a part of a larger movement to mainstream women's rights in human rights discourses. The collective message of these international organizations, across the security, democracy, political economy, and human rights subfields is increasingly clear: Gender equality should be a political priority not only because it is an important end in and of itself but also because it will improve the changes of reaching other important political goals, such as peace, democracy, economic stability, and human well-being.

Feminists, then, have asked why this remains true. Why, despite increasing awareness of gender discrimination, does it continue? Why, when the majority of the world's governments consider women equal to men, are women drastically underrepresented in governance? Why, when many indicators show that including women in economies would not only benefit women but also the economies more generally, do women remain on the margins of most economies around the world, including developed ones? Why are women's human rights lagging so far behind men's?

These questions bring us to the second feminist argument that gender should be included in our studies of global politics—that the discrimination that women experience around the world is not incidental, but structural. Certainly, the boundaries of what we consider women capable of have broadened quickly over the last century. In the majority of places around the world, a century ago, women were discouraged from working outside of the home, encouraged to submit to their husbands, and formally barred from participating in politics, particularly voting. The remaining boundaries to women's full political, economic, and social citizenship are, at first glance, much less formidable at present: There is very little that women are considered incapable of in most places in the world, and even less that they are formally prohibited from doing. Still, these remaining barriers carry a threat that the former ones did not. The remaining barriers are complicated, fluid, difficult to understand, and often invisible. After all, up to this point, this chapter has posed something of a paradox, asking why women remain *so disadvantaged* in global politics when much of the world understands them to deserve the same opportunities as men. As Spike Peterson and Anne Sisson Runyan note, feminists observe,

> The seeming contradiction between rising international attention to ameliorating gender inequality—which is now seen by many UN agencies and many member states as a significant source of global political, economic, and social problems—and the deepening of global crises that are undermining this acknowledgment and its implementation.[10]

Part of the answer to that question is that still there are many people, institutions, and governments that do not believe women should get the same opportunities as men. Still, even the places that endorse gender equality, people, institutions, and governments come up radically short of providing women equal representation, opportunities, and access to resources.

Feminists in IR have argued that this is because the international arena, and the states that are a part of it, are, at their foundation, gendered. This argument is more complicated than the argument that women are overtly discriminated against. Instead, feminists have argued that states, international organization, and the international system "select for" characteristics associated with masculinity over characteristics associated with femininity, priorities which not only impact the distribution of women and men but also shape the theory and practice of political relationships between actors and structures in global politics.

The claim that states are masculine constructions is more complicated than observing that men usually govern states. As R. W. Connell (1995) argues, men being in charge of most states is both product and producer of state masculinity. Men lead states because states prize characteristics associated with masculinity in their leadership, and their organizational practices are structured in relation to masculine values. Ann Tickner describes this as evident in "the belief, widely held in the United States and throughout the world, that military and foreign policy are the arenas of policy making least appropriate for women."[11] Voters around the world select their leaders on the basis of characteristics associated with instrumentality (and masculinity) such as assertiveness, coarseness, toughness, aggressiveness, sternness, activeness, rationality, and confidence over characteristics associated with expressiveness (and femininity) such as warmth, gentleness, sensitivity, emotion, talkativeness, and cautiousness.[12] This prizing of characteristics associated with masculinity over characteristics associated with femininity is replicated at every level of global politics, from interpersonal interactions to interstate relations.

Feminist scholars noted that, in the time running up to the 2004 elections, John Kerry was portrayed by his Republican opponents as feminine, in contrast to the masculinity of the George W. Bush Administration. In a speech condemning the Iraqi invasion of Kuwait, George H. W. Bush challenged Saddam Hussein's masculinity, asserting that "real men" did not invade their neighbors by surprise at night. These gendered interactions, however, are not a product of post–Cold War politics alone. Instead, they can be found in many of history's great stories. The Trojan War was told as a massive interstate conflict inspired by the kidnapping of a beautiful woman, Helen. Joan of Arc's trial for heresy and witchcraft centered around her insistence on participating in activities previously reserved for men and her refusal to comply with gender-stereotypical expectations of her behavior.

Scholars looking to understand the role of gender in global politics, then, have investigated how the international system and the global economy contribute to the subordination of women and other subjugated groups. This has involved observing the gendered nature, and rethinking, of traditional concepts in IR such as security, sovereignty, and globalization. Feminists have examined how hierarchical structures of class, race, and gender cross and intersect with national boundaries as well as the interactive effects of these hierarchies on the workings of global politics and economics. Importantly for feminists, in these investigations, gender is an analytical tool rather than just a descriptive category. By analyzing the gendered nature of global politics, feminists have put together a program of research that argues that gender is necessary, conceptually, to understanding global politics; crucial to explaining the causes and effects of events in global politics; and essential to constructing workable solutions to the world's most serious problems.

Many Feminist Approaches to IR

When we talked about gender above, we discussed that there was not just one experience of gender in the world and not just one approach to feminism. The same is true of feminist work in IR. This book, like most IR textbooks, is divided into different (and often conflicting) "paradigmatic" approaches to the discipline. One is either a realist or a liberal or a constructivist or something else. Rarely (but sometimes) do scholars attempt to combine paradigmatic approaches to the discipline, but usually, these are understood as in opposition to each other.

Feminist approaches to IR, however, are not like other paradigmatic approaches. One is not either a realist or a liberal or a constructivist or something else or a feminist. Instead, different feminists have approached IR in different ways. Many of them build on, but go beyond, some of the IR perspectives discussed in other chapters in this book. IR feminists, as discussed above, share an interest in gender equality or gender emancipation. Still, what feminists mean by those words does differ, as does their understanding of the right tools and methods to use to study gender in global politics. Feminists have generally categorized these approaches as feminist liberalism, feminist constructivism, feminist critical theory, feminist poststructuralism, and feminist postcolonialism.[13] I have also argued that there is such a thing as feminist realism, characterized by an interest in the role of gender in strategy and power politics between states, but other feminist approaches to the study of global politics are much more developed (2009). This section will briefly discuss the contributions of these different approaches.

Feminist Liberalism

Feminist work that has been classified as liberal in IR calls attention to the disadvantages that women have as compared to men in global politics and argues that the key to addressing this subordination is including women in the structures of global politics. Much like the more general liberal feminism discussed above, feminist liberalism in IR documents the various aspects of gender discrimination in IR. Liberal feminist work has documented the particular problems of women refugees, the causes of income differences between women and men, and human rights violations that happen to women disproportionately. They look at women's representation in the institutions and practices of global politics, and how their presence or absence affects the content of international politics. Liberal feminists focus removing legal barriers and other obstacles to women's access to the opportunities men take for granted.

Liberal feminists have also understood gender as a variable in explaining states' foreign policy choices. For example, Mary Caprioli and Mark Boyer (2001) have argued that states with higher levels of domestic gender equality were less likely to participate in international conflicts. While a number of other feminists are critical of the state-level focus of liberal feminists and their tendency to think of sex and gender as synonymous, this research program has contributed to the study of gender and IR by suggesting that phenomena that other IR theorists have explained without reference to gender (such as states' likeliness to make war) can be better explained by taking account of gender. Feminists of the liberal variety in IR have recently embarked on a large data-collecting project called the WomanStats database (www.womanstats.org), using quantitative and qualitative data to look for where and how gender affects the operation of international politics, which now contains dozens of indicators of women's status in 174 countries.

Feminist Constructivism

Feminist work from a constructivist focuses on the ways that ideas about gender shape and are shaped by global politics. Constructivist feminists study the processes by which ideas about gender influence global politics as well as the ways that interactions between states shape ideas about gender. For example, Jessica Peet (2010) argues that ideas about what women should be influence global policy making about human trafficking, while human trafficking norms shape expectations about women's behavior.

Another example of feminist constructivist work is Elisabeth Prugl's (1999) book, *The Global Construction of Gender*, which uses a feminist constructivist approach to analyze the treatment of home-based work in international law. Prugl shows that poor working conditions and low pay for home-based work have often been justified by characterizing home-based work as different than "real work." Noting that most people who work based in their homes are women shows that home-based work is less valued because ideas about femininity and womanhood have spurred the association of home-based work with the feminine, private sphere. This association, Prugl argues, was particularly salient in the debate about the International Labor Organization's Homework Convention. Prugl characterizes gender as a factor that influences the distribution of power in global politics, where things (like home-based work) associated with femininity have less power and prestige than things (like capitalist trade) associated with masculinity.

Feminist Critical Theory

Feminist critical theory explores the ideational and material manifestations of gendered identity and gendered power in world politics. Jill Steans explains the foundations of feminist critical theorizing:

> *Feminist critical theorists* are trying to find a way forward with retains both gender as a category of analysis and retains the historical commitment to the emancipatory project in feminism, but which takes on board the postmodern and postcolonial critique of the exclusionary practices of Western feminism.[14]

Many critical feminists build upon, but go beyond, the work of Robert Cox, a critical IR scholar who portrays global politics in terms of the interactions between material conditions, ideas, and institutions in production relations, the state-society complex, and world orders.[15] Critical feminist theorizing suggests that understandings about gender are only partly about how women experience life. The meaning that we give to those experiences also defines gender. Ideas that men and women have about their relationships to one another are an important part of the meaning of gender in social and political life.

A book called *In Service and Servitude* (1998) by Christine Chin uses a critical feminist perspective to study foreign female domestic workers in Malaysia. Chin examines the trend of immigration of underpaid and often exploited domestic workers from the Philippines and elsewhere into Malaysia, with emphasis on the boom in the 1970s. Chin argues that the traditional explanations for such immigration, which focus on wage differentials, are inadequate to explain this particular case, which featured both unique social dynamics between employer-families and a substantial amount of state regulation. Chin instead points out that the importation of foreign female domestic workers was supported and encouraged by the Malaysian state, despite slavery-like working conditions, as a part of a policy strategy to win the support of middle-class families interested in using those workers to show their improving social status. Chin shows that families (particularly women) in Malaysia perceived the ability to employ and abuse foreign (women) workers as a symbol of having attained a particular socioeconomic position in society. Chin's study, though, consistent with critical theorizing in IR more generally, does not stop at demonstrating how material gender discrimination interacts with ideas about gender roles. Instead, feminist critical theorizing identifies existing power relations with the intention of changing them.

Feminist Poststructuralism

Poststructuralist theory more generally focuses on meaning as it is embedded in language. Feminist poststructuralism argues that gendered language, particularly when certain words and traits are associated with masculinity and certain words and traits are associated with femininity, serves to empower the masculine and marginalize the feminine. While some people do not put a lot of stock in the meaning and use of words, feminist poststructuralists argue that our words tell us how we see the world, and even what the world is. Feminist poststructuralists are interested in the relationship between knowledge and power. They point out that, in the discipline of IR, men have traditionally been the "knowers," or the writers of the text from which we are supposed to learn and by which we are supposed to be inspired to do our research. For example, about a year ago, Steve Walt, a prominent IR scholar, blogged about the ten best books in IR. Not one of those ten books (or any of the books given an "honorable mention" in the post) was authored by a woman. Poststructuralist feminists argue that what counts as knowledge in IR has not only been *by* men, it has also been *about men*, particularly, about elite men's experiences in the public sphere. They point out that women have been cast aside both as knowers and as the subject of knowledge in global politics.

An important implication of this work is that gendered dichotomies that frequently appear in the work of IR scholars, like strong/weak, rational/emotional, public/private, civilized/uncouth, order/anarchy, and developed/underdeveloped, have been important not only in how we explain the world but also in what the world has become. Feminist poststructuralists emphasize that gender hierarchies are real but constantly changing and evolving with social contexts. Deconstructing these hierarchies is necessary in order for us to see them clearly, and to construct a less hierarchical international arena.

Two examples of feminist poststructuralist work might help to make sense of the approach. The first is a book called *Manly States* published in 2001 by Charlotte Hooper. Hooper claims that it is difficult to understand interstate interactions unless we see that mostly men conduct them. In an analysis of the *Economist*, Hooper examines texts, graphs, photos, and advertising material to conclude that the magazine is full of indicators that it and the political and economic institutions it reports on both value traits and representations associated with men and masculinity. Hooper shows that gender metaphors and gendered claims are pervasive and meaningful in global politics.

Another example of feminist poststructuralist work is Laura Shepherd's (2008) *Gender, Violence, and Security*, which evaluates United Nations Security Council Resolution 1325, passed in 2000, to address gender issues in conflict areas. Shepherd argues that the language of the Resolution is not just a reflection of the world it was written for, but also a way to organize and understand that world. She argues that the words of Resolution 1325 influenced its implementation. For example, Shepherd points out the number of places in Resolution 1325 where women are portrayed as passive victims of violence and/or advocates for peace. She argues that these portrayals still subordinate women, even in a Resolution ostensibly interested in women's empowerment and emancipation. If this is true, then, Shepherd contends that it becomes easier to explain the United Nations' continued inability to transform peace processes to be gender-inclusive. Shepherd's work suggests that paying attention to the gendered discourses of global politics is essential to understanding what global politics is like, and how effective solutions to global problems can be forged.

Feminist Postcolonialism

Postcolonial feminism focuses on the power relationships between diverse feminist perspectives around the world, arguing that colonial relations of domination and subordination are replicated in gender relations, and even in relationships between feminists in global politics and in the academic field of IR. Postcolonial theorists claim that the dominating relationships that colonizer states established over colonized states during the era of imperialism did not magically disappear when the colonized states became independent. Instead, they are interested in how part of the world continues to dominate the rest of the world, and how the First World constructs how we know and understand the Third World. Postcolonial feminists make similar claims about the way Western feminists have constructed knowledge about non-Western women.

Just as feminists have been critical of IR for generalizing men's experiences to women's lives, postcolonial feminists are critical of Western feminists for generalizing Western women's experiences to women around the world. Postcolonial feminists are concerned that Western feminists assume that all women have similar needs with respect to emancipation, when, in fact, their realities are very different. For example, sometimes Western feminists have ideas about women's human rights that do not resonate with many "Third World" women's perceptions of their needs and/or wants. Postcolonial feminists challenge western portrayals of "Third World" women as poor, undereducated, victimized, and lacking in agency. Recent work in postcolonial feminist IR, including that of Lily Ling and Anna Agathangelou, has explained gender subordination as at the intersection of gender, race, and culture, and blurring the boundaries between politics and political economy. Seeing these complexities, postcolonial feminist work seeks to redress gender subordination sensitive to cultural context.

These multiple approaches to the study of gender and global politics have much to contribute to understanding IR, individually and collectively. The final two sections of this chapter explore some of those contributions in the areas of security and political economy.

Putting It All Together: Gender and Security

What does it mean to be secure? What does it mean to be insecure? Is security different for individuals than it is for states? Is it different for states than it is for the world as a whole?

Feminists interested in security have made a number of contributions to this area of study. They have questioned the role of states as security providers. Feminists have argued that some states achieve security by sacrificing the security of their citizens or of other states. People whose security is sacrificed are often those at the margins of social and political life. Feminist scholars' commitment to ending gender subordination is consistent with a definition of security that is broad and centers around the individual. Feminist research has shown that the core concepts used to understand international security, such as the state, violence, war, peace, and even security itself, are gender-biased and urge redefining those core concepts in a less biased way. Feminist scholars have learned about the roles of women in war and in post-conflict reconstruction. They have identified gender-biased language and assumptions in nuclear strategy, the noncombatant immunity principle, peacekeeping policies, and military planning. In addition to providing critical views on the traditional ideas used to understand security, feminists have also discovered new areas for fruitful research, including the prevalence of sexual violence in war and women's soldiering.

Feminists pay attention to the fact that the opposite of "security" is "insecurity" and look for the ways that women are insecure as a starting point for understanding security. Women are insecure when they are poor, when they do not have access to health care, when they are victims of domestic violence, when they do not have adequate employment, when they are victims of rape, and when their responsibilities outweigh their resources. It follows that threats to women's security (and to security more generally) include, but are not limited to, poverty, inadequate health care, domestic violence, sexual violence, and unemployment. Because of this, in place of the focus on states that fight wars, feminist scholars' analysis of security begins with the lives of people, particularly women, at the margins of global politics.

This perspective has inspired feminist work on gender's relationship to a variety of topics that have been of interest to those who study security, such as gender mainstreaming, peacekeeping, the movement of people, noncombatant immunity, terrorism, women's violence, human security, environmental security, transitional justice and post-conflict reconstruction, peace advocacy, militaries and militarism, and the theory and practice of security more generally. Though feminists who work on security do so from a variety of perspectives, there are several common arguments of Feminist Security Studies.

The first common argument mentioned briefly above is a broad understanding of who should get to be "secure" and what that security entails. In this view, everyone, regardless of power or status, deserves to be secure—a concept which includes not only freedom from war and interstate violence, but also from domestic violence, rape, poverty, disease, ecological destruction, and gender subordination. Recognizing that states, which are "secure," often have many insecure women in them, feminist scholar Cynthia Enloe argued that "the personal is international and the international is personal."[16]

Enloe was arguing that our lives matter to international security and that international security matters to our individual lives. Caron Gentry and I wrote about this when we researched on women's violence in global politics. Living in an area where there is an intransigent conflict impact woman who committed acts of martyrdom for the Palestinian cause. They also impact international security, not only through their acts of martyrdom but also in their other political involvements and economic and social relationships. Feminist scholarship about security studies how people affect international security, and how international security affects people. These things are of interest not only for elite decision makers in international politics, but also for "normal" people, like soldiers, corporations, and even readers of this text.

A second common argument of feminist studies of security politics is that the international security realm prizes values associated with masculinity over values associated with femininity. If this is true generally in global politics, it is truer in the security realm, where feminists have linked masculinism and militarism. Masculinism is the idea that it is justified and natural to live in a world with gender hierarchy. States want their militaries to evince values of bravery and courage, their leaders to be decisive and rational, and their states to be independent and strong—all characteristics associated with masculinity. On the other hand, states find emotion, interdependence, and vulnerability, characteristics associated with femininity, undesirable. Feminist scholars have found states prioritizing masculinity over femininity in their choices of weapons,[17] in their war strategies,[18] in their choices of leaders,[19] and in conflicts they choose to engage in and ignore.[20]

A third common theme in Feminist Security Studies is the importance of gender in analyzing security. It is one thing to say that gender "matters" in global politics; it is another to argue that global politics cannot be effectively understood without reference to gender. Feminists who study security often make the second argument. They argue that many of the things that we take for granted in the security world—like deterrence, military power, private military corporations, and nuclear weapons—would not exist in their current form without patriarchy in global politics. They also point out that gender can be a causal variable in states' security decisions. For example, feminist scholars have pointed out that, sometimes, states' foreign policy choices are guided by their identities, which are based on associations attached to manliness. Feminist Security Studies argue that gender "adds something" to the study of security but also that it is a transformative force. They argue that the study of security would be fundamentally different if it asked questions about gender.

This leads to a final common tenet for Feminist Security Studies: that the omission of gender from scholarship that studies security does not make that work gender-neutral. Not mentioning gender does not make it go away. Instead, the supposed irrelevance of gender to international security is wrong in two senses—it's wrong because it ignores women, and it's also wrong because it provides an inaccurate picture of how global politics generally and global security specifically work.

These tenets of Feminist Security Studies have been employed in a wide variety of research agendas over the last decade. Nicole Detraz (2009) argues that environmental security is intrinsically linked both to women's safety and to gendered perceptions of security. Susan Wright (2010) argues that the negotiations surrounding the development of the Biological Weapons Convention prioritized masculine notions of security. Swati Parashar (2010) has studied the media's gendered portrayals of male and female fighters in the conflict in Kashmir, particularly as they relate to issues of national identity. Jennifer Heeg Maruska (2010) has studied the different traits associated with masculinity that different leaders in U.S. foreign policy emphasize, focusing on episodes of what she identifies as hypermasculinity in foreign policy choices. Christine Sylvester (2010) has focused on the sense and sensuality elements of war and conflict, which have been ignored by traditional studies of international security but cannot go unnoticed when security is studied from the perspective of individual women's lives.

Gender and Political Economy

Why is it that women represent 70 percent of the world's people living in poverty? What does it mean to have economic stability? How do international structures interact with local structures to produce or disturb that stability? Is economic stability something people (or states) only gain at the expense of others?

As I mentioned before, women constitute the majority in poverty around the world. The percentage of women living in rural areas who can be classified as impoverished is actually rising, not dropping. Women who work for wages are generally poorly paid, and many women do home, care, and agricultural work that goes unpaid. Women have not been left out of the economic reforms planned by the IMF and the World Bank, but their gender is often invisible to the planners and implementers of these policies.

Feminist perspectives on global political economy (GPE) are investigating the extent to which these disturbing trends should be blamed on gender discrimination. They are interested in the causes of women's, and other marginalized groups', economic insecurities and potential solutions to these problems. Feminist work in political economy has recognized what scholars have identified as the gendered division of labor in global politics and analyzed its impacts.

The gendered division of labor in modern times can be traced to the Industrial Revolution in Europe, where definitions of what it means to be a man and what it means to be a woman were shaped around the growing division of work to be done *at work* (man) and work to be done *at home* (woman). The notion of a "housewife" developed, where women's work was seen as private, domestic, and the property of the family, and the public world of the market was populated by rational, economically oriented men. Despite the fact that more and more women have come to work outside the home in recent times, the association of women with housework, caregiving, and mothering remains strong.

When women do go into the workforce, they are overrepresented in the caring professions (teaching, nursing, daycare, service industries) and underrepresented in the financial industries and capital trade. To the extent that women choose these professions, they do not choose them on the basis of profit maximization (which is what traditional economic theory assumes) but instead based on social expectations of what women should be and what they should do. Cynthia Enloe (1989) has claimed that a "modern" global economy requires "traditional" ideas about women.

Ideas about gender also often lead to women having double responsibilities. Women who work outside the home continue to do the majority of the care work inside the home while being paid less than men with comparable qualifications for their workforce duties. Care labor often requires time and energy that would otherwise be spent on paid labor. Women often sacrifice professional opportunities to care for children and elderly relatives.

The narrow definition of "work" as work in the waged economy tends to make it difficult to see many of women's contributions to the global economy. Feminists have argued that the gendered division of labor cannot be understood without reference to political, economic, and social choices based on assumptions about gender. Feminist work about the GPE has made a number of observations to highlight the importance of gendered forces.

For example, feminists have highlighted some gendered economic forces, like the global sex trade,[21] that are often ignored by political economists. Feminists have studied gender representations in the movie and beauty industries.[22] They have pointed out that the gendered divide between the "public" realm and the "private" realm obscures the work women do. Feminists have also argued that, in addition to neglecting women generally, conventional work in political economy has also underestimated women's economic agency.[23]

Several feminists have also attempted to understand the gendered nature of globalization. V. Spike Peterson (2003) has divided the globalized economy into three sectors. The "productive" sector is the thing we usually think of as the global economy—where goods and services are made and traded. The "virtual" economy is the trade in intangible things, like money and information. The third sector, to which Peterson gives equal weight as the other sectors, is the reproductive economy. The reproductive economy includes pregnancy, parenting, household maintenance, elderly care, and socialization. Feminists argue that these three categories taken together are more suited to finding women and gendered structures in the GPE, and a more accurate reflection of how the world works more generally.

Feminists have also asked about how the GPE would function if we restructured it taking women's labor and women's experiences into account. They have looked in unconventional places, like households, sweatshops, and camp towns, for economic knowledge. These inquiries have led feminist to suggest restructuring the health care industry on the basis of care.[24] Feminists have also argued against the treatment of sexuality as a commodity. They have suggested that women's unpaid labor be recognized not only intellectually but also financially. Feminists have suggested that the gendered structure of the political economy and the gendered distribution of resources in the global economy require attention not only among feminist scholars but also in IR more generally. They argue that we cannot understand the GPE without reference to gender.

Gendering IR: Looking Forward

One question that this chapter must still ask is: What now? If we have figured out that gender "matters" in global politics, and have examples from security and political economy, then what do we do with that knowledge? How do we learn more? How do we study gender in global politics? And how do we end gender subordination?

At the beginning of this chapter, I asked if the world would be different if women ran it as a way of asking you to think about gender in global politics. Many feminists in IR, however, find another question more interesting: Would the world be different if the power structures of global politics and global economics valued characteristics of femininity over characteristics associated with masculinity? Or valued gender-associated traits equally?

Feminist work in IR provides a clear perspective on this question, arguing that one of the defining, structural, and foundational properties of global politics is gender hierarchy, particularly, valorizing the masculine at the expense of the feminine. Feminists have argued that this feature is constant over time and space and that one cannot understand the global political arena without understanding the role that gender plays in it, whatever paradigmatic approach one uses to look at IR.

Wrap-Up

Here is the take-home message. Feminism is an approach to global politics that demonstrates the necessity of taking account of gender to understand what the world is, what is going on in the world, and how to fix the world's problems. Feminist research shows that gender matters to how people's everyday social lives work, both "at home" and on a global scale. Therefore, gender is crucial, conceptually, to understanding what global politics is, and important, empirically, to seeing the causes and consequences of policy choices in global politics. Because gender is an important factor in global social and political life, it is an important perspective to pay attention to when looking to improve the world that we live in. Taken together, these insights and the research that produces them help us understand how global politics functions, and how we might go about changing it.

Further Reading

1. Cynthia Enloe, *Nimo's War, Emma's War: Making Feminist Sense of the Iraq War* (2010), is a deep and incisive feminist analysis of the Iraq War through the lives of eight women (four Americans, four Iraqis) which is at once cutting-edge and accessible. It does a good job of showing how feminist theoretical insight can be applied to "real-world" analysis.
2. Laura Sjoberg, "Introduction to *Security Studies*: Feminist Contributions" (2009), provides an introduction to the concepts and methods feminists use to analyze international security, and what their contributions are. The remainder of the (summer 2009) special issue of *Security Studies* and the following edited volume (*Gender and International Security: Feminist Perspectives*, ed. Laura Sjoberg) contain a number of examples.
3. J. Ann Tickner, "You Just Don't Understand: Troubled Engagements between Feminists and International Relations" (1997), lays out some of the successes and troubles in the relationship between feminist work in IR and the IR "mainstream." Tickner's *Gendering World Politics* (2001) also discusses these issues, and what it means to be a feminist in IR, in depth.
4. Hilary Charlesworth, Christine Chinkin, and Shelley Wright, "Feminist Approaches to International Law" (1991), translates some of these issues specifically to what we look at and how we look at it when we study international law and international jurisprudence. It draws parallels between feminisms in IR, feminisms more generally, and potential applicatory strategies.

5. Brooke Ackerly, Jacqui True, and Maria Stern, eds., *Feminist Methodologies for International Relations* (2006), provides a discussion of how to do feminist research in IR methodologically and the assumptions about how we know and what we know inherent in researching through feminist lenses. It includes the viewpoints of a number of the leading scholars in the field.
6. J. Ann Tickner and Laura Sjoberg, eds., *Feminism and International Relations: Conversations about the Past, Present, and Future* (2011), grapples with the evolution and contributions of feminist work to the field of IR in its first twenty years and asks difficult questions about the future of feminist research in the field through a series of conversations across scholarly generations.
7. V. Spike Peterson, "Political Identities/Nationalism as Heterosexism" (1999), is a sophisticated analysis which extends the theoretical insights of feminisms in IR to think about questions of (hetero) sexuality in the theory and practice of global politics, linking hetero-orthodoxy to nationalism and the practices of war and conflict.
8. Lene Hansen, "Gender, Nation, Rape: Bosnia and the Construction of Security" (2001), applies feminist theorizing to the question of the conflict in Bosnia in the 1990s, illustrating the relationships between gender, nationalism, sexual violence, and our perceptions of security.

Notes

[1] See discussion in Laura Sjoberg, "Introduction to *Security Studies*: Feminist Contributions," *Security Studies* 18 no. 2 (2009): 183–213.
[2] Cynthia Enloe, *Bananas, Beaches, and Bases: Making Feminist Sense of International Politics* (Berkeley: University of California Press, 1989), 11.
[3] Alexandra Cawthore, "The Straight Facts on Women in Poverty." Center for American Progress, October 8, 2008, accessed December 28, 2009, http://www.americanprogress.org/issues/2008/10/women_poverty.html.
[4] UNIFEM. "Women, Poverty, and Economics." United Nations Development Fund for Women, Gender Issues Publications. 2009, accessed December 28, 2009, http://www.unifem.org/gender_issues/women_poverty_economics/.
[5] Amnesty International, "Violence against Women," *AI Bulletin* 12 no. 2 (November 20, 2009).
[6] Laura Shepherd, *Gender, Violence, and Security: Discourse as Practice* (London: Zed Books, 2008); Sjoberg, "Introduction to *Security Studies*."
[7] Nadje Al-Ali and Nicola Pratt, *What Kind of Liberation? Women and Occupation in Iraq* (Berkeley: University of California Press, 2009).
[8] Soumita Basu, "Security through Transformations: The Case of the Passage of UN Security Council Resolution 1325 on Women and Peace and Security," Thesis submitted in Fulfilment for the Degree of PhD, Department of International Politics, 2009.
[9] K. Nakray, "Gender Budgeting: Does It Work? Some Experiences from India," *Policy and Politics* 38 no. 2 (2009).

[10] V. Spike Peterson and Anne Sisson Runyan, *Global Gender Issues*, 3rd Edition (Boulder, CO: Westview Press, 2009), 6.

[11] J. Ann Tickner, *Gender in International Relations: Feminist Perspectives on Achieving Global Security* (New York: Columbia University Press, 1992).

[12] Leonie Huddy and Nadya Terkildsen, "Gender Stereotypes and the Perception of Male and Female Candidates," *American Journal of Political Science* 37 no. 1 (1993): 119–47.

[13] See J. Ann Tickner and Laura Sjoberg, "Feminism," in *International Relations Theories: Discipline and Diversity*, eds. Steve Smith, Tim Dunne, and Milja Kurki (Oxford: Oxford University Press, 2006).

[14] Jill Steans, *Gender and International Relations: An Introduction* (New Brunswick, NJ: Rutgers University Press, 1998), 29, emphasis in the original.

[15] Robert Cox, "Social Forces, States, and World Orders: Beyond International Relations Theory," in *Neorealism and its Critics*, ed. Robert O. Keohane (New York: Columbia University Press, 1986).

[16] Cynthia Enloe, *The Morning after: Sexual Politics at the End of the Cold War* (Berkeley: University of California Press, 1993).

[17] Lauren Wilcox, "Gendering the Cult of the Offensive," *Security Studies* 18, no. 2 (2009): 214–40.

[18] Carol Cohn, "Sex and Death in the Rational World of Defense Intellectuals," *Signs: Journal of Women in Culture* 12, no. 4 (1987): 687–718.

[19] Yvonne Due Billing and Mats Alvesson, "Questioning the Notion of Feminine Leadership: A Critical Perspective on the Gender Labelling of Leadership," *Gender, Work & Organization* 7, no. 3 (2000): 144–57.

[20] Laura Sjoberg, *Gender, Justice, and the Wars in Iraq* (New York: Lexington Books, 2006).

[21] Jacqueline Berman, "(Un)Popular Strangers and Crises (Un)Bounded: Discourses of Sex-Trafficking, the European Political Community, and the Panicked State of the Modern State," *European Journal of International Relations* 9 no. 1 (2003): 37–86.

[22] Angela McCracken, "Playboy Cosmopolitanism, Sexy Girls-Next-Door, and Latin America." Paper presented at the Annual Meeting of the International Studies Association, February 15–18, New York, 2009.

[23] J. K. Gibson-Graham, *The End of Capitalism (As We Knew It): A Feminist Critique of Political Economy* (Minneapolis: University of Minnesota Press, 2006); Angela McCracken, "Gender and Globalization," in *International Studies Encyclopedia*, ed. Robert Denemark (London: Blackwell, 2010).

[24] Fiona Robinson, *Globalizing Care: Ethics, Feminist Theory, and International Relations* (Boulder: Westview Press, 1999).

Works Cited

Ackerly, Brooke A. 2000. *Political Theory and Feminist Social Criticism.* Cambridge: Cambridge University Press.

Ackerly, Brooke, Maria Stern, and Jacqui True, eds. 2006. *Feminist Methodologies for International Relations.* Cambridge: Cambridge University Press.

Al-Ali, Nadje, and Nicola Pratt. 2009. *What Kind of Liberation? Women and Occupation in Iraq.* Berkeley: University of California Press.

Basu, Soumita. 2009. "Security through Transformations: The Case of the Passage of UN Security Council Resolution 1325 on Women and Peace and Security," Thesis submitted in Fulfilment for the Degree of PhD, Department of International Politics.

Berman, Jacqueline. 2003. "(Un)Popular Strangers and Crises (Un)Bounded: Discourses of Sex-Trafficking, the European Political Community, and the Panicked State of the Modern State." *European Journal of International Relations.* 9, no. 1: 37–86.

Caprioli, Mary, and Mark Boyer. 2001. "Gender, Violence, and International Crisis." *Journal of Conflict Resolution.* 45, no. 4: 503–18.

Card, Claudia. 1996. "Rape as a Weapon of War." *Hypatia.* 11, no. 4: 5–17.

Charlesworth, Hilary, Christine Chinkin, and Shelley Wright. 1991. "Feminist Approaches to International Law." *American Journal of International Law.* 85, no. 4: 613–45.

Chin, Christine. 1998. *In Service and Servitude: Foreign Female Domestic Workers and the Malaysian "Modernity" Project.* New York: Columbia University Press.

Cohn, Carol. 1987. "Sex and Death in the Rational World of Defense Intellectuals." *Signs: Journal of Women in Culture.* 12, no. 4: 687–718.

Confortini, Catia. 2010. "Links between Women, Peace, and Disarmament: Snapshots from the WILPF." In Laura Sjoberg and Sandra Via, eds. *Gender, War, and Militarism: Feminist Perspectives.* New York: Praeger Security International.

Connell, R. W. 1995. *Masculinities.* Berkeley: University of California Press.

Cox, Robert. 1986. "Social Forces, States, and World Orders: Beyond International Relations Theory." In Robert O. Keohane, ed. *Neorealism and its Critics.* New York: Columbia University Press.

D'Amico, Francine, and Peter R. Beckman. 1995. *Women in World Politics: An Introduction.* Westport, CT: Bergin and Garvey.

Detraz, Nicole. 2009. "Environmental Security and Gender: Necessary Shifts in an Evolving Debate." *Security Studies.* 18, no. 2: 345–69.

Due Billing, Yvonne, and Mats Alvesson. 2000. "Questioning the Notion of Feminine Leadership: A Critical Perspective on the Gender Labelling of Leadership." *Gender, Work & Organization.* 7, no. 3: 144–57.

Elshtain, Jean Bethke. 1987. *Women and War.* New York: New York University Press.

Enloe, Cynthia. 1989. *Bananas, Beaches, and Bases: Making Feminist Sense of International Politics.* Berkeley: University of California Press.

Enloe, Cynthia. 1993. *The Morning after: Sexual Politics at the End of the Cold War.* Berkeley: University of California Press.

Enloe, Cynthia. 2010. *Nimo's War, Emma's War: Making Feminist Sense of the Iraq War.* Berkeley: University of California Press.

Gibson-Graham, J. K. 2006. *The End of Capitalism (As We Knew It): A Feminist Critique of Political Economy.* Minneapolis: University of Minnesota Press.

Hansen, Lene. 2001. "Gender, Nation, Rape: Bosnia and the Construction of Security." *International Feminist Journal of Politics.* 3, no. 1: 55–75.

Heeg Maruska, Jennifer. 2010. "When are States Hypermasculine?" In Laura Sjoberg, ed. *Gender and International Security.* London and New York: Routledge.

Hooper, Charlotte. 2001. *Manly States: Masculinities, International Relations, and Gender Politics*. New York: Columbia University Press.

Horn, Denise. 2010. "Boots and Bedsheets: Constructing the Military Support System in a Time of War." In Laura Sjoberg and Sandra Via, eds. *Gender, War, and Militarism: Feminist Perspectives*. New York: Praeger Security International.

Huddy, Leonie, and Nadya Terkildsen. 1993. "Gender Stereotypes and the Perception of Male and Female Candidates." *American Journal of Political Science*. 37, no. 1: 119–47.

Hudson, Heidi. 2009. "Peacebuilding through a Gender Lens and the Challenges of Implementation in Rwanda and Cote d'Ivoire." *Security Studies*. 18, no. 2: 287–318.

Kaufman, Joyce, and Kristen Williams. 2007. *Women, the State, and War: A Comparative Perspective on Citizenship and Nationalism*. New York: Lexington Books.

MacKenzie, Megan. 2009. "Securitization and Desecuritization: Female Soldiers and the Reconstruction of Women in Post-Conflict Sierra Leone." *Security Studies*. 18, no. 2: 241–61.

McCracken, Angela. 2009. "Playboy Cosmopolitanism, Sexy Girls-Next-Door, and Latin America." Paper presented at the Annual Meeting of the International Studies Association, February 15–18, New York.

McCracken, Angela. 2010. "Gender and Globalization." In Robert Denemark, ed. *International Studies Encyclopedia*. London: Blackwell.

Moon, Katharine. 1997. *Sex among Allies: Militarized Prostitution in U.S.-South Korea Relations*. New York: Columbia University Press.

Nakray, K. 2009. "Gender Budgeting: Does It Work? Some Experiences from India." *Policy and Politics*. 38, no. 2.

Parashar, Swati. 2010. "Women, Militancy, and Security: The South Asian Conundrum." In Laura Sjoberg, ed. *Gender and International Security: Feminist Perspectives*. London and New York: Routledge.

Peet, Jessica. 2010. "Combatting Human Trafficking: Creating Security or Constructing Gender?" Paper Presented at the 2010 Annual Meeting of the Southern Political Science Association, January 2–6, Atlanta, Georgia.

Peterson, V. Spike. 1999. "Sexing Political Identities/Nationalism as Heterosexism." *International Feminist Journal of Politics*. 1, no. 1: 34–65.

Peterson, V. Spike, and Anne Sisson Runyan. 2010. *Global Gender Issues*, 3rd Edition. Boulder, CO: Westview Press.

Prugl, Elisabeth. 1999. *The Global Construction of Gender: Home-Based Work in the Political Economy of the 21st Century*. New York: Columbia University Press.

Robinson, Fiona. 1999. *Globalizing Care: Ethics, Feminist Theory, and International Relations*. Boulder: Westview Press.

Shepherd, Laura. 2008. *Gender, Violence, and Security: Discourse as Practice*. London: Zed Books.

Sjoberg, Laura. 2006. *Gender, Justice, and the Wars in Iraq*. New York: Lexington Books.

Sjoberg, Laura. 2009. "Introduction to *Security Studies*: Feminist Contributions." *Security Studies*. 18, no. 2: 183–213.

Sjoberg, Laura, ed. 2010. *Gender and International Security: Feminist Perspectives*. New York and London: Routledge.

Sjoberg, Laura, and Caron Gentry. 2007. *Mothers, Monsters, Whores: Women's Violence in Global Politics.* London: Zed Books.

Steans, Jill. 1998. *Gender and International Relations: An Introduction.* New Brunswick, NJ: Rutgers University Press.

Sylvester, Christine. 2010. "War, Sense, and Security." In Laura Sjoberg, ed. *Gender and International Security: Feminist Perspectives.* London and New York: Routledge.

Tickner, J. Ann. 1992. *Gender in International Relations: Feminist Perspectives on Achieving Global Security.* New York: Columbia University Press.

Tickner, J. Ann. 1997. "You Just Don't Understand: Troubled Engagements between Feminists and IR Theorists." *International Studies Quarterly.* 41, no. 1: 611–32.

Tickner, J. Ann. 2001. *Gendering World Politics.* New York: Columbia University Press.

Tickner, J. Ann, and Laura Sjoberg. 2006. "Feminism." In Steve Smith, Tim Dunne, and Milja Kurki, eds. *International Relations Theories: Discipline and Diversity.* Oxford: Oxford University Press.

Tickner, J. Ann, and Laura Sjoberg, eds. 2011. *Feminism and International Relations: Conversations about the Past, Present, and Future.* London and New York: Routledge.

Wilcox, Lauren. 2009. "Gendering the Cult of the Offensive." *Security Studies.* 18, no. 2: 214–40.

Wright, Susan. 2010. "Feminist Theory and Arms Control." In Laura Sjoberg, ed. *Gender and International Security: Feminist Perspectives.* London and New York: Routledge.

CHAPTER 7

Postmodernism

Rethinking the Study of International Relations

Rosemary E. Shinko

Postmodernism asks us to think about how the current structure and organization of the study and practice of international relations (IR) limits our ability to effectively respond to global issues. Postmodernists argue that we are unable to productively address pressing problems related to immigration, refugee populations, violence, and the emergence of a seemingly endless war on terror because we continue to rely on patterns of thinking that remain trapped within realism and liberalism. Postmodern approaches reject the argument that IR is little more than the repetition of natural and unalterable patterns of action, as the more mainstream theories of realism and liberalism would have us believe. What makes postmodern approaches so interesting is the fact that they actively try to envision the world as other than it is at present by calling into question our assumptions about what IR is all about. It is a form of critique that aims to make us question the ways we think and act in order to help us realize that our world could be different.

In between realism's acceptance of the tragic necessity of war, on the one hand, and liberalism's belief in one universally shared set of values and norms, on the other, postmodernism acknowledges that there are different forms of life, different types of political community, different normative commitments and value structures, all of which, they believe, reflect the complexity and diversity of human life itself. Postmodernism rejects oversimplification, striving instead to provide a much more complex and detailed view of international issues and events. Such an approach to the study of IR offers an open-ended inquiry which literally takes on the entire discipline, reformulates its key questions, restructures its conversations, and at the end of the day, offers new intellectual pathways for thinking about ourselves and the world we want to create. Thus, this chapter and its theoretical perspective is one of the more difficult for an undergraduate to comprehend, but once embraced, it provides a whole new perspective on the global events that shape your world.

Thinking Like a Postmodernist: The Social and Political Context

Viewing the world through a postmodernist frame of mind entails a shift in focus from accepting what has come to be expected or regarded as natural. Pauline Rosenau refers to this new way of thinking as "re-setting the codes one normally employs in social science analysis, turning around one's thought processes."[1] For instance, most of us might share a fundamental belief that there really is only one right way to view international politics and that there is only one true version of international events that we should be able to arrive at after much study and analysis. A postmodern frame of mind resets this code, this belief in one correct or true answer, by offering us competing versions of international events.

The first step in thinking like a postmodernist is to reject overly simplified explanations that try to reduce very complex international events down to a few simple reasons, like the realist contention that war is a natural condition of human existence and that it can be attributed to the fact that we live in an anarchical world without a centralized authority that could prevent it. To reflect on the recent ISIS-inspired terror attacks from a postmodern frame of mind would require the critical capacity to examine the perspectives of those who support such attacks and the networks through which these types of attacks draw inspiration and direction, to study the political, social, and economic contexts, to reflect on the military interventions and drone attacks carried out by the United States in the global war on terror, and to consider the historical patterns of the use of force and violence to attempt to secure the interests of various political actors. Where each political actor sits in relation to the issues raised above influences how they perceive the causes and consequences of the ongoing war on terror and how they justify and explain their responses and actions. A postmodernist could, for example, analyze the decision by the United States to launch the global war on terror in response to the 9/11 attacks and inquire as to why this was deemed the natural or rational response. Or a postmodernist could investigate the claim that they, meaning the terrorists, hate our way of life in order to examine how we determine who is civilized or who is barbaric. Postmodernists refuse to accept singular explanations that create stark, overly simplified contrasts between our way of life and theirs. In sum, postmodernism refuses to accept realism's fatalism that this is the way the world is or liberalism's optimism that progress and freedom rest on the creation of a shared, singular worldview, led by the West.

There is no concise, standard definition of what postmodernism means, and this is partially why this approach to studying IR can be confusing. It is basically a diverse collection of ideas, themes, and concepts that try to make sense of the rapid and disorienting changes that we see happening in the world around us. It also is not a theory in the way in which you have come to understand the term in connection with realism, liberalism, or Marxism, for example. Theories represent rather coherent, streamlined, and objective patterns of thought that attempt to explain how the world works.

Postmodernists, however, raise serious questions about IR theory because they do not believe that we can separate ourselves from our social and political contexts and study international events as if they were separate, objective entities. Therefore, postmodernists accept a natural level of subjectivity that other theories believe can be avoided. In this regard postmodern approaches pick up on constructivist themes, in that we live in an intersubjective world of our own making. For postmodernists our world is made up of a diversity of issues and a multiplicity of voices that represent different thoughts, hopes, and desires. Thus, postmodernism is not a theory but a collection of themes, ideas, and concepts that can be loosely grouped under the term, postmodern.

What ties all of these approaches together under the term postmodern is a shared recognition that the world is undergoing a series of complex and destabilizing changes and shifts that have ushered in a sense of crisis. This sense of crisis reflects the belief that more traditional and commonly accepted ways of trying to make sense of the world are not only inadequate but also quite possibly dangerous. Thus, postmodern approaches recognize that fundamental aspects of our lives continue to be profoundly altered from the shifts ushered in by rapid technological changes in communication, access to information, digital photographic imagery, the speed with which information travels, and capitalism's ever-morphing and expanding network of economic connections. One thing postmodern approaches are acutely aware of is that these shifts and changes are not necessarily benign, progressive, or emancipatory. In other words, all of these technological developments, for example, can be viewed positively as we witnessed the use of Facebook, Twitter, and cell phone linkages to spark, coordinate, and empower democratic movements like the one that toppled the Mubarak regime in Egypt; however, they also possess a darker side that can be harnessed by those in power to track, monitor, silence, and detain protesters in nascent democracy movements in China and elsewhere. Thus, we cannot label the technological advancements as definitively good or bad but must be aware of their multiple interpretations.

Postmodern Perspectives and Attitudes

Postmodern scholars could be said to share certain attitudes and perspectives that inform the work they do and the approaches they take to the study of IR. Loosely configured, these ideas can be said to represent the worldview of postmodernism which includes the realization that there is no one single, sovereign version of the truth. Truth is multiple, and we would be better served if we spoke about truth in the plural as truths. Postmodernists reject the assertion that there is one fundamental version of truth that is timeless or true for all people everywhere.

They view the commitment to a singular view of truth as a very dangerous way of thinking that has been used to justify genocide, racism, colonialism, and other violent patterns of exclusion and marginalization. Postmodernists recognize the fact that people will hold competing versions of truth (truth claims) and that they may in fact not be ultimately reconcilable. A good example of this would be the debate over the hijab, the form of dress worn by some Muslim women that covers their hair and neck and/or those other forms of dress, which either covers their entire body including their faces or merely reveals their eyes. The French government has taken a position that such a form of dress violates the fundamental principles of secularism, the separation of religion and the public realm, and equality. Such a form of religiously motivated dress sets Muslim women apart from the rest of French society and privileges one specific religious form of dress over others. Thus, the government's response has been to prohibit outward displays of religious attire for all French citizens in public schools and public places. What has been seemingly settled by the dictate of state law has, however, not been settled on a more interpersonal level. Muslim women who chose to veil their bodies do so out of their own sense of religious convictions and identity, while those who regard such an expression of Muslim identity as threatening and politically provocative refuse to compromise. What is evident here is indeed the existence of competing truth claims that take different approaches to the question of citizenship and how citizens of a certain state may literally appear in public.

Thus, the space in between different truths must be left open, and individuals must be free to explore various claims to truth for themselves. In conjunction with this, you will find postmodernism associated with terms like multiplicity, pluralism, and hybridity. Hybridity, in particular, indicates the belief in an intellectual mindset that values differing points of view and reveals a willingness to borrow from and combine a variety of competing perspectives. This sense of competing truths and the value placed on things like hybridity is what distinguishes this perspective from more traditional theories. There is no sense of a universal human nature or a standard interpretation of anarchy. It is the diversity of how we might view the world that makes postmodernism so engaging.

You will hear postmodernism described as anti-foundationalist and this too represents one of the crucial features of such an approach. It derives from their view of the multiplicity of truth because a foundation represents a singular base upon which an entire theory can be built. Think about the foundations created by realism and liberalism. Realism begins with the foundational presumption that international politics is a struggle for power among states to secure their national interests. Liberalism agrees with realism that political actors are self-interested, but that they can create an alternative to the constant struggle for power and security through cooperation. What postmodernists question is the way in which both realism and liberalism have been founded on the power and authority of the sovereign state in combination with the belief in the autonomy and sovereignty of the individual.

Critiquing Sovereignty

The key to understanding postmodernism's rejection of the current foundations of IR can be found in its critique of sovereignty in the work of Richard Ashley and R. B. J. Walker, Cynthia Weber, and Jens Bartelson.[2] These scholars wondered how we came to regard sovereignty as the inevitable foundational base of international politics. The common understanding of sovereignty is that it refers to the ability to decide for oneself. Sovereignty also involves the belief in a supreme, independent, and final center of authority. Think for a moment about the implications of an entire system of international politics founded on the concept of sovereignty. Based upon a realist perspective, such a system presumes the timelessness of the state and expects political actors to use power to secure and maintain their own interests and security, above all other considerations.

The postmodern critique of sovereignty questions the ways in which the modern sovereign state attempts to establish, maintain, and control the national identity of its own citizens. It is also a critique of the ways in which we have come to regard the individual as sovereign, autonomous, rational, and possessing a fully formed and complete sense of identity. What is so typically postmodern about this critique of sovereignty, however, is that it poses sovereignty as a question and asks how sovereignty became the accepted foundation of IR.

Postmodernism views sovereignty as a disciplinary center that attempts to control us by identifying us first and foremost as particular citizens of a particular state. Postmodernists want to understand the practices that make us national citizens and bind us to national territorial boundaries. It asks, "How do we become citizens that learn how to bear allegiance to a set idea of national identity, how to resist those who would challenge our national identity, and most importantly, how to defend this identity with our very lives?"

One of the more injurious and troubling effects of sovereignty's disciplinary and productive power can be viewed in relation to the construction of identity and difference in IR.[3] Due to the fact that our identities as citizens are produced around the concept of the sovereign state and the sovereign individual, we privilege our national identity as well as strive to maintain a sense of uniformity and sameness in our domestic identities within the state. Thus, what it means to be American is bound up in attempts to represent a unified external image to the rest of the world while also creating an internal image that reflects what it means to be a real or true American. This striving for a settled expression of identity is problematic for postmodernists because it is built upon political decisions about who does or does not belong in our community, which privileges some at the expense of others. All you need to think about are the political battles being waged over identity in France and the ways in which Muslim citizens have been marginalized and disadvantaged in their ability to secure jobs and political access. And you can also think about the political battles being fought in America over immigration and whether or not Hispanic Americans will be fully accepted as real Americans because, as Samuel Huntington concludes, the American dream can only be dreamt in English by those who draw their heritage from the White, Anglo-Saxon cultural tradition.[4]

Postmodernists don't agree with realist arguments about the inevitable tragedy inherent in the conduct of international politics because we create the concepts and ideas that support the foundations that make and sustain our world. Thus, it wasn't human nature or the inevitability of the tragic repetition of events that resulted in colonization, the holocaust, or the use of nuclear weapons against Japan but the creation of a political foundation based on sovereignty that made such independent, autonomous decisions possible. If one begins from a foundation based upon a selfish, self-centered, autonomous actor who uses power to secure his or her own interests, postmodernists would argue that you are creating the very dynamic of fear that you then come to view as natural, as reality. In short, are political actors naturally fearful, autonomous, and self-centered or are they that way because we have defined them to be so? Thus, sovereignty may not be the most effective way to organize our international political system, but the problem, and a problem that we need to critically examine.

Critiquing Metanarratives

Along with the view that truth is plural and the emphasis is on the continuous questioning of foundations comes the postmodern assertion that we can no longer rely on overarching universal explanations (metanarratives) that attempt to explain how the world really is. Rather they maintain that the world is full of diverse, local, and multiple stories and that there is no way to capture all of this complex diversity in one singular theory or explanation. For example, Islam is a religion that has over one billion followers worldwide and has as great internal diversity and complexity as that found within Christianity. However, in the minds of some Westerners, Islam has been reduced to an association with radical fundamentalism and a desire to impose Sharia law and its way of life on the world. Such an attempt to paint all followers of Islam as radical, violent fundamentalists is merely an effort to establish the Christian religious tradition as the correct, true, or good and to dismiss Islam as invalid, false, or evil. Such a stringent dichotomy is inherently dangerous because it not only oversimplifies different worldviews but also sets up the choice between the two as merely an objective exercise analogous to answering a true/false question on an exam. This is ultimately akin to saying that you are either with the terrorists or with us.

Postmodernists reject such oversimplifications and draw our attention to the ways in which we actively participate in interpreting, describing, and creating meaning in how we talk about and discuss world events and issues. In practical terms, they conclude that there is no one theory that can explain international affairs. This of course makes us responsible for recognizing and trying to understand a wide array of perspectives. We are not outside world events and issues. We are actively engaged in them and can only discuss them from our own location and particular point of contact and personal involvement. Our world is an intersubjective one that we create together, not something that we can study like an experiment in a petri dish. It is not one made up of independent, sovereign actors but individuals who are born into a highly interactive and interpersonal social context. We live embedded in a diverse and complex web of human relationships.

That is why postmodernists view our individual identities as plural, shifting, ever changing and that we are always in the process of becoming. And as we move through our lives and in and out of various interactions with others, we realize that our identities are multiple and constantly open to change. We are students, siblings, members of community groups, religious congregations, members of fraternities or sororities, all of which intersect to form various aspects of our identity, but no one singular aspect of our overall identity can be captured by just describing us in terms of one of these connections. These connections will then, in turn, be supplanted by other connections as we move into new identities as partners, parents, employees, bosses, and so various parts of our identities shift and take on new meanings and social implications as we progress throughout our lives. It is a never-ending process of change and a layering of various identities—social, political, economic, and/or cultural. Think about how you behave and how you view the world within different social settings and at different points in your life. How you view a conflict in the world is different if you are the sibling or spouse of military personnel that may be deployed as opposed to the child of a left-leaning family unit that only espouses peace. And how you view that conflict might differ depending on whether you are eighteen or fifty years old. The idea is that all of these interpretations are in a state of flux and dependent on different aspects of someone's identity.

Ethical Relationships

These realizations are crucial to understanding how postmodern IR scholars are approaching the ethical relationships between self and other. This relationship is described by the use of the term *alterity*, which refers to individuals who are just different from the self. When postmodernists use the term *Others*, they are drawing attention to the realization that we can never really know someone else and that there will never be a way to absolutely define them or to fully understand them. Postmodernists also reject the idea that we can know others by comparing them to ourselves and then making certain assumptions or drawing certain conclusions about them based on our own lives, thoughts, or actions.

Postmodern IR has been keenly aware of the differences that separate self from other, but they are also keenly aware how often our history has presented us with violent responses to those who were labeled as the other, different, and threatening. The response to otherness has included attempts to eliminate it (the holocaust or the extermination of indigenous peoples), assimilate it (attempts to allow women to participate in various aspects of political and economic positions of power by demanding they become just like men), or to marginalize it (dismissing demands for equality and justice by disregarding the ability of minority groups to even make claims in the first place). Postmodernists are searching for alternative ways to respond to difference that will be more productive, inclusive, and expansive.

Thus, they begin by approaching ethics in IR from the perspective that ethics is something we engage in, something we practice. Therefore, they are not interested in creating a theory of ethics that can be objectively established and universally applied but rather context-specific understandings of ethical relations. The question for them is how to encourage us to explore the possibilities for an ethics of encounter that doesn't include rigid preconceptions about the identity of the other nor presumes that our own identity is stable and fixed.[5] The ethical spaces between self and other need to be worked through as a result of an engagement that proceeds from openness and not from a sovereign foundation based upon the presumption of fear and violence.

Deconstruction and Genealogy

Deconstruction and genealogy are two of the most recognizable approaches used by postmodernists to critically analyze language and historical narratives. One of the most distinctive aspects of postmodern work in IR is its focus on discourse and how language constructs not only our world but also our own sense of self (subjectivity) and how we fit into the world. Thus, postmodern forms of analysis draw attention to the role language plays in creating our social context. There is also an emphasis on the fact that language brings things into existence because it performs a labeling function that identifies what things are or who one is.

Thus, using the term freedom fighter as opposed to terrorist not only serves to distinguish one type of individual from another but also brings that type of identity into existence, attaches it to a certain individual, and dictates how we should respond. A freedom fighter is located within a community as a supporter and defender of that entity, but a terrorist is the exact opposite and represents an existential threat to the existence of the community. The key political determination rests on whom or what may threaten the survival of a community and how we identify who and what those threats are. For IR postmodernists analyzing language patterns and the ways in which different terms are used forms an important part of their efforts to understand how we determine political, social, and economic threats.

Deconstruction

Deconstruction, which is associated with the French philosopher Jacques Derrida,[6] exposes the ways in which language creates structures of differentiation and that terms are often set up in binary pairs of opposites. In these pairings of terms, one is always set above the other as more important or simply better. There is an inherent value structure that undergirds these discursive pairings, and they are accompanied by an attempt to separate and distance the more unwanted or derogatory traits by associating them with the lesser or weaker term. For instance, think of the pairing male/female and the words that are most commonly associated with each side of this pairing. Male is denoted by the terms strong, rational, objective, while female is associated with terms such as weak, emotional, subjective. What the structure of the pairings attempts to indicate is that the meanings are diametrically opposed. In other words, one is viewed as better than the other.

The key is to notice how those occupying the stronger side of the pairings deliberately attempt to disassociate themselves from what they find as unwanted characteristics within themselves. So they work very hard to push those undesirable characteristics onto others while constructing a false sense of superiority around themselves. The point is to learn how to recognize when language is being used to accomplish this social positioning and to show how and why it is a construction by picking apart the way words are strung together to reveal the deliberate efforts to claim a superior position (deconstruction). Meaning making is something that humanity actively participates in and postmodernists deliberately draw attention to the political struggles over what things mean.

Francis Fukuyama, in an article in *Foreign Affairs*, argued that male "attitudes toward violence, power and status . . . are rooted in biology" and that they are not the product of social construction.[7] You may or may not find this biological argument convincing, but what underlies it are his very negative views on feminism. Consider the following quotes:

> Most important, the task of resocializing men to be more like women— that is, less violent—will run into limits. What is bred in the bone cannot be altered easily by changes in culture and ideology. Some feminists talk as if gender identities can be discarded like an old sweater, perhaps by putting young men through *mandatory gender studies* courses when they are college freshmen [emphasis added]. Male attitudes on a host of issues, from child-rearing and housework to "getting in touch with your feelings" have changed dramatically in the past couple of generations due to *social pressure* [emphasis added]. But socialization can accomplish only so much and efforts to *fully feminize young men* will probably be no more successful that the *Soviet Union's efforts* to persuade its people to work on Saturdays on behalf of the heroic Cuban and Vietnamese people [emphasis added].[8]

What deconstruction does is to first draw your attention to the negative aspects of feminization, the term he repeatedly uses throughout the article to refer to the increasing participation of women in world politics. Look at the key phrases italicized above and how he associates feminism with forcing men to become more feminine through compulsory courses and cultural practices. And for good measure, he links it to Soviet communism in order to bring in the moral threat feminism poses to individual (male) freedom.

He also provides a visual aid on page 29 of a flapper-era woman with large boxing gloves who has just knocked a man down to the ground. And the caption reads "Beating men at their own game: A woman floors her beau, 1910." The photograph achieves two aims. It demonstrates that women do indeed desire to dominate men and, including the photo in the context of the language previously cited, helps to confirm that this is what we have to fear about feminist IR. Feminist IR has now been associated with communism, compulsion and social pressure, and as virtually subverting nature itself. If you have never read the groundbreaking work of J. Ann Tickner and her response to Fukuyama you might be inclined to accept this portrayal as accurate.[9] But what deconstruction makes you realize is that every argument creates its own internal hierarchy of value and Fukuyama clearly wants to convince you that feminists in IR are not only morally wrong but also politically dangerous, because of their efforts to feminize politics in alignment with their natural biological desire to compromise instead of standing and fighting like real men.

Genealogy

Genealogy takes its cues from Nietzsche, *On the Genealogy of Morals*, and Michel Foucault, *Discipline and Punish*. It focuses on the ways in which history is written and how certain versions of history come to be regarded as true. Thus, genealogy begins in the present and asks how we got to this current point where certain ideas are accepted as true and certain ways of speaking and thinking are regarded as rational.

Postmodernists view history as a narrative of events, ideas, and concepts that we write, and as we are writing it, there are struggles over what should be included or excluded. There are controversies over what particular things mean or should mean but as history is being written, these disagreements are settled, and we are presented with a linear version of history. But postmodernists are highly skeptical of historical narrative precisely because of the ways in which it leaves other voices, other perspectives, and other stories out of its own grand narrative. Think about how you learned European history as one straight story line from the Greeks and Romans through the European Enlightenment to the hegemonic position of the United States. Postmodernism disrupts this narrative by drawing attention to other stories that encompass different but significant political, cultural, and economic developments.

The intellectual and cultural achievements of the Muslim world is a perfect reason why other historical stories should be incorporated into our present understanding of the past. There has been a complex cultural exchange between the east and the west and both played a significant role in the development of our present intellectual and cultural heritage. In short, postmodernists think about history not as an inevitable story of progress but as a story of complex, hybrid intermixing that does not necessarily reveal a linear march to a greater or more advanced understanding of who or what we are.

Genealogy reveals how history comes to reflect the superiority of a certain dominant and more powerful perspective. Thus, as Nietzsche argues, history is about the "will to power" a struggle over what things mean and whose version will ultimately triumph. You can easily see an example of this type of struggle in the conflict between the Israelis and the Palestinians. The Israelis attempt to write a version of history that presents an uninterrupted three-thousand-year claim to their homeland and that Jerusalem is not a settlement but a birthright. Palestinians attempt to write a counternarrative that draws attention to the daily existence of Palestinians in the census records compiled by the British and all of the traces of their communal life, which have somehow been written out of the history of the Middle East. So genealogy draws attention to these competing visions of history in order to indicate how the power to narrate history is bound up with how we come to regard our knowledge of the past as true and incontrovertible.

As the dominant narrative is retold over and over again and reconfirmed as the truth, those not part of this story are pushed to the margins of history or forgotten altogether. Postmodernists want to know how power operates to marginalize and discredit certain perspectives and points of view while validating and securing others. Thus, history is contingent and is the result of political choices and not, as we have come to believe, an objective account of reality.

Putting It All Together I: Immigration and the Greek Debt Crisis

Consider for a moment about how you think about security. What does it mean to be secure, and how do we achieve it? Within the realist paradigm, you can never really be secure because it is a self-help international system. But you can improve your chances of achieving some semblance of security by gaining more power than other actors. The acquisition and maintenance of power, whether you think of it in economic, military, or political terms, is key. Liberalism rests its hopes for security on international institutions, laws, norms, and procedures that create an interdependent, web-like structure to constrain and channel the actions of international actors toward the peaceful resolution of conflicts. Feminists, constructivists, and postmodernists all critique this narrow understanding of security, albeit from slightly different vantage points. Alexander Wendt, a constructivist theorist, believes that anarchy only exists because we came up with the concept and then used that idea to create an international system of insecurity that states struggle within and against.[10] Feminists argue for a broader understanding of security and for feminist scholars like J. Ann Tickner and Jill Steans, the gendered structure of international politics is what makes both women and men insecure.[11] Postmodernists like Anthony Burke deconstruct the concept of security to reveal the ways in which a state-centric view of security creates a political situation where security can only be achieved by making someone else insecure. Thus my security comes to rest on "the insecurity and suffering of an-*Other.*"[12] The question for postmodernists is how to make the insecurity of others not only visible but also ethically important enough for us to pay attention and respond.

Security is an organizing principle that draws political, social, and economic forms of power together. In other words, states were originally founded on a promise to secure those inside its territory against those who would threaten its order and control, whether from within or without. Security functions as both a promise and as "a defining condition of human experience and modern political life."[13] Thus, Burke urges us to pay attention to how our lives are politically, socially, and economically organized around the safety and security of the state. He further asks us to think about how we have come to regard others as "resources for [our own] use and exploitation." And finally, he insists that we try to understand "how death and suffering can . . . be seen as necessary and productive, as perhaps regrettable but not immoral." In short, we are asked to think about the ways in which our "security, prosperity and freedom" are purchased at the expense of the "insecurity and dying of others."[14]

The European immigration crisis and the Greek debt crisis provide the perfect opportunity for us to explore these troubling aspects of modern security and their direct connections to political economy. For postmodernists, security and political economy are intertwined and the rising tide of migrants and refugees trying to make their way to Europe via Greece, in conjunction with the Greek debt crisis, has resulted in a perfect storm of economic hardship, vulnerability, and insecurity. What is important for postmodernists is to draw attention to the various aspects of insecurity and to identify who is being made insecure and why.

Greece acknowledged that it had an unsustainable level of debt and found itself on the verge of bankruptcy in spring 2010. With no other options, Greece negotiated three bailout packages all of which imposed stringent austerity measures and led to debt in the billions. In addition to the ongoing economic recession, Greece also found itself struggling with an almost unprecedented flow of refugees from the Middle East and Northern Africa. Greece has become one of the main arrival points for those fleeing economic deprivation and violence in their home countries in search of security and opportunity in Europe. The death toll is unprecedented in terms of the thousands of lives lost for those attempting to cross the Mediterranean Sea, and things are becoming even more precarious for those who have made it ashore due to the rising power of anti-immigration parties like Golden Dawn.

A postmodernist would be interested in examining the various narratives or stories being told about who is vulnerable and why. It is easy to see a hierarchy of pain and suffering emerging that pits Greek citizens against refugees and migrants. There also is a hierarchy of pain and suffering privileging Greece's creditors and the wealthier northern European economies over the ordinary Greek citizens who have been hardest hit by rising taxes, unemployment, and imposed austerity measures including deep cuts in social services and benefits. As a result, there have been dramatic increases in hunger, homelessness, poverty, depression, and suicide across Greek society. Postmodernists would explore how these vulnerabilities cut across various layers of society where populations, across Europe, Northern Africa, and the Middle East, have been rendered vulnerable by the political, social, and economic power of national and global elites. There also is a narrative or a story that Europe tells about itself that stresses its values of humanity, its support for human rights, and its commitment to solidarity. It is this narrative, being used by those advocating that Europe has a moral obligation to respond to what has become the most severe refugee crisis since World War II, that would also be a point of interest for postmodern scholars. The key for a postmodernist would be to draw all of these competing discourses together (including, e.g., those involving national political leaders, international and regional organizations, local community, and humanitarian groups) and to trace how these discourses inform and become embedded in various political, social, and economic policies.

Postmodernists would also be interested in exploring the ways in which both the Greek debt crisis and the immigration crisis have been discussed in terms of controlling the threat or contagion from spreading throughout Europe creating a domino effect across other troubled economies in Italy, Spain, or Portugal and their potential negative impacts on the healthier and wealthier parts of the continent. Postmodernists might choose to ask about neoliberal economic power and how Greece's three bailouts will be used. Will Greece find itself further impoverished? And how can it grow its own economy if saddled with deepening debt and punishing austerity measures? Postmodernists would deconstruct the whole concept of economic threat in order to examine how these threats are constructed in terms of the interests of the most powerful and advantaged segments of the global economic structure.

The same holds true for the immigration crisis and the rising popular sentiments against what is referred to as the Islamization of Europe. So postmodernists would analyze how parties such as Golden Dawn in Greece or the Northern League in Italy stress the themes of invasion and promote the idea that they, not the refugees and migrants, are in dire need of protection. The response of the European governments has been to attempt to contain the contagion at the border before it even gets to the shores of Europe. Thus, postmodernists would question the militarization of the immigration crisis and the repercussions of European governments treating this problem as a security issue. They would examine the implications of refugees and migrants being subjected to a host of border controls, profiling, and the use of naval forces to block the flow of people across the Mediterranean. Thus, we need to understand how security *here* has become dependent on suffering *there* and how these political, social, and economic discourses of threat rest on various social constructions of *who* and *what* is to be feared.[15]

Putting It All Together II: The London Transport Bombings

Another interesting contemporary example of postmodern critique that questions how meanings get constructed around the concept of fear is found in the work of Cindy Weber.[16] Weber looks at how the website Werenotafraid.com tries to restore order in the minds of the British public in the wake of the London transport bombings in July 2005. The website attempts to confirm the public's lack of fear by posting declarative statements such as "we are not afraid to ride public transportation," "we are not afraid to walk down a crowded street," and "we are not afraid of each other."[17] Citizens were encouraged to add their own postings and photographs to the "we are not afraid" website and as Weber argues, these efforts were directed at "championing Reason over the irrationality of fear as well as morality over the exercise of power as vengeance."[18]

The "we are not afraid" website also operates as a call to unity for all Britons to "stand together, united by a single, timeless message of resistance to fear and resistance to the irrational vengeance it inspires. The path to British security, then, is unity."[19] What you should notice according to Weber is how hard the website is working to attach fearlessness to what it means to be British and to attach the term irrationality to fear itself. The fear that is most irrational is the fear of terrorism, and Weber discusses how the website urges ordinary people to go about their daily activities without fear of terrorism. However, a subsequent posting on the website pictured a woman's face, veiled all except for her dark eyes looking slightly to her left. The words "we are afraid!" encircle her face.

Weber explains that the young woman, Samera, also included the following posting to accompany her picture. "This pic is to highlight my concern as an INNOCENT (capitalized in the original) muslim and to raise awareness about the increase in racial hate n crime because of the atrocity in London last week."[20] And then Weber proceeds to deconstruct the connection between irrationality/fear/unity that the website tried to create and attach to what it means to be British. What Weber reveals is how Samera's picture and posting reveal someone who "not only stands outside the community of the like-minded who are not afraid but it also proclaims the existence of another 'we'—the 'we' who are afraid."[21] Furthermore, her posting reveals that it is indeed very rational to be afraid under the current circumstances in London, especially if you are Muslim. What is also interesting is how a response to Samera's posting encourages "Samera . . . stand beside us . . . and don't be afraid," which as Weber argues confirms that Samera is outside what it means to be British, because she is asked to stand beside, not with or inside, the British community.[22] Cindy Weber's focus on these web postings demonstrates exactly how postmodernists attempt to disrupt what we think might be natural by drawing on viewpoints that are not necessarily part of the main centers of power in an attempt to encourage us to question and critique those very same centers of power.

Thus, what Weber demonstrates is how the concept of fearlessness is attached to certain presumed notions of what it means to be British and to be part of the unified community where fear of terrorism is regarded as irrational. And yet Samera's voice reveals the voice of a different community not part of the British conception of unity that challenges the very meaning of fearlessness. You can see the political efforts to attach moral superiority to the linkages established between rational /British unity/fearlessness and the ways in which these sets of meanings are attached to a particular ideal type of British community. The whole point of this postmodern analysis is to reveal the internal tensions surrounding the concept of fear, but one thing it will not do for you, however, is to provide a resolution for the tensions it exposes.

Wrap-Up

Postmodern approaches to the study of IR are first and foremost a critical engagement with what we assume to be true and or commonly accepted about IR. Its aim is to shake up our sense of certainty that we really know how the world is and who we definitively are. It requires of us a willingness to question our attachments to a sovereign political entity, like the state, as the final and ultimate arbiter of our identities, freedoms, and life chances. Postmodern approaches want to make what seems rational, clear, and straightforward somehow strange and open to dispute and doubt. It puts a lot of pressure on the individual to be responsible for initiating these changes in thought and action, because at the end of the day, this shift in perspective rests with the self.

But even more than being a radical thought experiment, postmodern approaches encourage us to critique the ways in which power operates and to create spaces for resistance. In this regard they encourage us to create relationships with others across the global community, with whom we share a sense of struggle against restrictive and oppressive systems of power. This entails working below, through, and above the state to craft ethical relations sensitive to the marginalized, the dispossessed and the excluded. But the important thing to remember is that postmodernism strives to maintain spaces for difference to flourish so solidarity is not conceived as a Western project to save the rest of the world. No, it is best thought of as a working together with respect for cultural difference, local context, and specific historical circumstances.

Further Reading

1. Amy Allen, "Ethics and Post-Structuralism" (2010), provides an introduction to Foucault's understanding of power and subjectivity and Derrida's approach to deconstruction. The author also discusses the ethical significance of their scholarship.
2. Richard Devetak, "Post-structuralism" (2009), is an excellent resource for students who want to explore postmodernism/post-structuralism in more depth. The chapter presents a wide range of contemporary postmodern/post-structural authors and a comprehensive review of their critical engagements with the state and the concept of the political.

3. Michel Foucault, *Discipline and Punish* (1995), is a good place to begin your exploration of Foucault's work on power, discipline, and knowledge. It is key to understanding his view that power operates within/across a web of relationships and how we learn to discipline ourselves so that we fit into existing structures of power.

4. Stephens, A. C., "'Seven Million Londoners, One London': National and Urban Ideas of Community in the Aftermath of the 7 July 2005 Bombings in London 155" (2007), is a postmodern analysis of events following the London transport bombings in July of 2005. It is an interesting analysis to read in conjunction with Cindy Weber's article referenced in this chapter. Stephens's article focuses on how terror attacks prompt us to rely on ideas of community that stress unity and exclusionary political practices.

Notes

[1] Pauline Marie Rosenau, *Post-Modernism and the Social Sciences* (Princeton, NJ: Princeton University Press, 1992), 8.

[2] Richard K. Ashley and R. B. J. Walker, eds. "Introduction: Speaking the Language of Exile: Dissidence in International Studies," Special Issue of *International Studies Quarterly* 34, no. 3 (1990); Richard K. Ashley and R. B. J. Walker, eds. "Conclusion: Reading Dissidence/Writing the Discipline: Crisis and the Question of Sovereignty in International Studies," Special Issue of *International Studies Quarterly* 34, no. 3 (1990); Cynthia Weber, *Simulating Sovereignty Intervention, the State and Symbolic Exchange* (Cambridge, UK: Cambridge University Press, 1995); and Jens Bartelson, *A Genealogy of Sovereignty* (Cambridge, UK: Cambridge University Press, 1995).

[3] See William Connolly, *Identity\Difference: Democratic Negotiations of Political Paradox* (Ithaca, NY: Cornell University Press, 1991), for a more detailed discussion of this effect.

[4] Samuel Huntington, "The Hispanic Challenge," *Foreign Policy* (March/April, 2004): 30–45.

[5] David Campbell and Michael J. Shapiro, eds. *Moral Spaces: Rethinking Ethics and World Politics* (Minneapolis, MN: University of Minnesota Press, 1999).

[6] Jacques Derrida, *Of Grammatology* (Baltimore, MD: Johns Hopkins University Press, 1997); and Jacques Derrida, *Writing and Difference* (Chicago, IL: Chicago University Press, 1978).

[7] Francis Fukuyama, "Women and the Evolution of World Politics," *Foreign Affairs* 77, no. 5 (September/October 1998): 27.

[8] Fukuyama, "Women and the Evolution," 27–28 and 36.

[9] J. Ann. Tickner, "Why Women Can't Run the World: International Politics According to Francis Fukuyama," *International Studies Review* 1, no. 3 (Fall 1999): 3–11.

[10] Alexander Wendt, "Anarchy Is What States Make of It: The Social Construction of Power Politics," *International Organization* 46, no. 2 (Spring 1992): 391–425.

[11] J. Ann. Tickner, *Gender in International Relations* (New York: Columbia University Press, 1992); and Jill Steans, *Gender and International Relations* (New Brunswick, NJ: Rutgers University Press, 1998).

[12] Anthony D. Burke, *Beyond Security, Ethics and Violence: War against the Other* (London, UK: Routledge, 2007), 28, emphasis in the original.

[13] Burke, *Beyond Security, Ethics and Violence*, 31.

[14] The three previous quotes are attributable to Burke, *Beyond Security, Ethics and Violence*, 13.

[15] Burke, *Beyond Security, Ethics and Violence*, 6.

[16] Cynthia Weber, "An Aesthetics of Fear: The 7/7 London Bombings, the Sublime, and Werenotafraid.com," *Millennium: Journal of International Studies* 34, no. 3 (2006): 683–711.

[17] Weber, "An Aesthetics of Fear," 685.

[18] Weber, "An Aesthetics of Fear," 687.

[19] Weber, "An Aesthetics of Fear," 694.

[20] Weber, "An Aesthetics of Fear," 700.

[21] Weber, "An Aesthetics of Fear," 701.

[22] Weber, "An Aesthetics of Fear," 703.

Works Cited

Allen, Amy. 2010. "Ethics and Post-Structuralism." In D. Bell, ed. *Ethics and World Politics*, 54–72. London: Oxford.

Ashley, Richard K., and R. B. J. Walker, eds. 1990. "Introduction: Speaking the Language of Exile: Dissidence in International Studies." Special Issue of *International Studies Quarterly*. 34, no. 3: 259–68.

Ashley, Richard K., and R. B. J. Walker, eds. 1990. "Conclusion: Reading Dissidence/Writing the Discipline: Crisis and the Question of Sovereignty in International Studies." Special Issue of *International Studies Quarterly*. 34, no. 3: 367–416.

Bartelson, Jens. 1995. *A Genealogy of Sovereignty*. Cambridge, UK: Cambridge University Press.

Burke, Anthony D. 2007. *Beyond Security, Ethics and Violence: War against the Other* London, UK: Routledge.

Campbell, David, and Michael J. Shapiro. eds. 1999. *Moral Spaces: Rethinking Ethics and World Politics*. Minneapolis: University of Minnesota Press.

Connolly, William. 1991. *Identity\Difference: Democratic Negotiations of Political Paradox*. Ithaca, NY: Cornell University Press.

Derrida, Jacques. 1997. *Of Grammatology*. Baltimore, MD: Johns Hopkins University Press.

Derrida, Jacques. 1978. *Writing and Difference*. Chicago, IL: Chicago University Press.

Devetak, Richard. 2009. "Post-Structuralism." In S. Burchill and A. Linklater, eds. *Theories of International Relations*, 183–211. New York: Palgrave Macmillan.

Foucault, Michel. 1995. *Discipline and Punish*. New York: Vintage Press.

Fukuyama, Francis. September/October 1998. "Women and the Evolution of World Politics." *Foreign Affairs*. 77, no. 5: 24–40.

Huntington, Samuel. March/April 2004. "The Hispanic Challenge." *Foreign Policy*. 30–45.

Nietzsche, Friedrich. 1989. *On the Genealogy of Morals and Ecce Homo.* New York: Vintage.

Rosenau, Pauline Marie. 1992. *Post-Modernism and the Social Sciences.* Princeton, NJ: Princeton University Press.

Steans, Jill. 1998. *Gender and International Relations.* New Brunswick, NJ: Rutgers University Press.

Stephens, A. C. 2007. "'Seven Million Londoners, One London': National and Urban Ideas of Community in the Aftermath of the 7 July 2005 Bombings in London 155." *Alternatives.* 32, no. 2: 155–76.

Tickner, J. Ann. 1992. *Gender in International Relations.* New York: Columbia University Press.

Tickner, J. Ann. 1999. "Why Women Can't Run the World: International Politics According to Francis Fukuyama." *International Studies Review.* 1, no. 3: 3–11.

Weber, Cynthia. 1995. *Simulating Sovereignty Intervention, the State and Symbolic Exchange.* Cambridge, UK: Cambridge University Press.

Weber, Cynthia. 2006. "An Aesthetics of Fear: The 7/7 London Bombings, the Sublime, and Werenotafraid.com." *Millennium: Journal of International Studies.* 34, no. 3: 683–711.

Wendt, Alexander. Spring 1992. "Anarchy Is What States Make of It: The Social Construction of Power Politics." *International Organization.* 46, no. 2: 391–425.

CHAPTER 8

Wrap-Up

What Should We Make of IR Theory?

Eric K. Leonard

We began this international relations (IR) theory journey with a goal—to provide you with the tools to better understand world politics. This book was seeking nothing more than that simple goal. The tools that you now have at your disposal are the theories of international politics. They are diverse, complex, sometimes competing, and hopefully helpful to your analysis of the world around you. However, as was stated in the first chapter, the journey to engage and understand these theoretical perspectives can sometimes be a bit overwhelming. If you are anything like the students in my classes, or me as an undergraduate for that matter, you would be a bit overwhelmed at this point in the semester. The past seven chapters have thrown a lot of new information, vocabulary, and fresh ways of seeing the world at you. This can certainly be a bit overwhelming. So let us stop to catch our breath and see if we can conclude this book with a very short recap of what we have learned, along with a moment to take stock of our original goal. In other words, let us see if you have the tools available to describe, understand, and predict events in world politics and then discuss how you might employ those tools.

Your Toolbox

Recall the goals of theory, as discussed in chapter 1: a theory should provide an empirical description of the world, an understanding of actor behavior, and, based on these initial two qualifications, some predictive capabilities. This book has examined several theories, although not nearly all the possible perspectives on international politics. These include realism, liberalism, Marxism, social constructivism, feminism, and postmodernism. Along with these six theories, the authors also discussed numerous subinterpretations of these broader theories. These include neorealism, complex interdependence, dependency theory, and many others. All of these theories have provided different ways in which students can analyze the complex world around them, and all have provided a lens of understanding.

In thinking back on these theories, it may just seem like a big jumbled mess of academic jargon and contrasting viewpoints. The purpose of this conclusion is not to recount all aspects of each theory, but instead to provide students with a way to make sense of the jumbled mess that this textbook has created. In order to clarify things a bit, let's provide a means by which to compare these theories. In other words, let's construct a list of attributes that each theory holds.[1] Creating such a list will provide students with a chart they can employ to compare the different perspectives and how they view the world. This should benefit students in their employment of each theory and assist them in seeing how each perspective may differ.

Now, although this section will create a list of guiding questions for each theory, it will not give you the theoretical specifics for each attribute. That would be too easy. I think that the best way for students to use this concluding chapter would be to complete a chart of sorts that provides a comparative model of IR theory. Therefore, the following paragraphs will list the attributes (key questions) and students should then fill in how each theory would answer the impending question.[2]

The first attribute students can compare is the primary cause of behavior. In other words, is what the theoretical perspective believes the main reason actors behave the way they do? Is it the structure of the system? Is it the economic underpinnings? Is it human nature? Students should now be able to determine what the primary causal factor is for actor behavior. One thing to be wary of when trying to answer this question is that more than one factor may exist for each theory. As a result, students should do their best to try and narrow that list and come up with the principal factor, if you can, in fact, identify one dominant factor. But in the end, some theories may not limit themselves to one simple causal factor because that cause could be socially constructed or indeterminate. Thus, students will need to identify this complexity and make note of it in their chart.

In order to identify the causal behavior of actors, it is obviously important to answer the question, who is the primary actor? Should we focus on states? Terrorist organizations? multinational corporations? intergovernmental organizations? All of the above? None of the above? Certainly, each theory has its own perspective on answering this question, and some may provide a more diverse list, reasoning that no one actor can claim greater influence over others. Thus, students should be careful in addressing this question and not limit themselves to only one actor for each theory.

Along with these two foundational attributes, when comparing the different theories, students must also consider what attributes each primary actor holds. Does the theory see each actor as being rational? And how would they define this term? It may seem obvious, but for many, the notion of rationality is a contestable term, and so you must consider it as such. Students should also ask if the actor is unitary. Meaning, do they act with one voice? Typically, this term is applicable when theories discuss states as the primary actor, but if the actor is not unitary, what does this mean for our understanding of world politics? Another question to consider when thinking about the attributes of international actors is whether they have fixed interests or do their interests change based on context or leadership? Addressing this question will bring students into the heart of the predictive capabilities of a theory, but at this point in your journey through IR theory, it should be apparent that not all theories see actor interests as fixed or static.

Finally, what is the resulting interaction amongst these actors? This is the point where all of the previous attributes are brought to bear on an analysis of the situation. If a student now understands who the primary actors are, what causes their behavior, and what attributes they hold, an analysis of their interaction with one another can occur. Simply put, students should be able to put the theory into practice and emerge with an accurate description, understanding, and possible prediction about world politics. This is exactly what we have been hoping to achieve, and the tools you now have at your disposal (the different IR theories) can assist in this goal.

Who Won?

This brings us back to one of the crucial questions raised in the introductory chapter—is one theory better than another? In other words, should you privilege one theory because you believe it has won the theory war? I would imagine that after studying these theories, you now understand the difficulty in declaring a particular theory victorious in its ability to describe, understand, and predict. This revelation brings us back to the notion of integrative pluralism, not disengaged pluralism.[3]

As discussed in the introductory chapter, it is best to approach IR theory as a discussion amongst the different theories (integrative pluralism) rather than a competition. Integrative pluralism can be defined as an approach that "accepts and preserves the validity of a wide range of theoretical perspectives and embraces theoretical diversity as a means of providing more comprehensive and multidimensional accounts of complex phenomena."[4] It seems a reasonable claim that world politics is constructed of complex phenomena and that there is a need to understand that phenomena. What integrative pluralism claims is that no one theory can truly capture that complexity, and therefore, the application of just one theory fails to provide a proper understanding of world politics.

Just think about some of the cases discussed in this book. Nike's labor policies, the formation of the ICC, the first Gulf War, the EU, a chemical weapons ban, and all the others. In each case, the authors made an argument that their theory provided an adequate explanation and understanding of the phenomena. However, for each case it appears that different theories provided different explanations. What this book is asking you to do is avoid boxing yourself into one theory and always trying to explain and understand world politics based on that one theory. Think about the phenomena you are studying and try all the theories and see which provides an accurate explanation and understanding. The theories are your tools, and it is important to employ the right tool for the right job. By doing so, your task will be easier and in the case of world politics, your understanding more accurate.

Wrap-up: Only the Beginning, Not the End

This brings us to the end of this book (I did say this was a short conclusion) but not the end of your journey. One problem students often perceive in an introductory-level class is a fragmented course content in which they see little or no connection from one section of the course to the next. Students see the class as several different but disconnected sections or topics. They fail to see the linkage from beginning to end. When talking about a typical Introduction to International Politics class, students see several different sections: theory, actors, issues, and maybe others depending on the instructor and the syllabus. After reading this text, what I am hoping students understand is that theory is the foundation of the course, and a proper understanding of world politics necessitates taking theory with you into the coming sections of the course.

I can hear my students now—"Oh crap, you mean I actually have to remember this stuff and apply it to the rest of the course? I had a hard enough time dealing with it the first time and now you are telling me we are going to be using it for the rest of the semester?" And my answer is always the same—"yes, because if you truly want to understand world politics then your toolbox must be filled with the knowledge of IR theory." I hope that you do not see this application of theory as a burden but as a means to understanding the world, because in the end, only a knowledgeable citizenry can create a better world. Good luck in your journey of world politics and remember, theory is neither a beginning nor an end, but a means to understanding.

Notes

[1] I use this list in my own classroom but do not claim such a catalog as unique. Most introductory textbooks have a similar list and over the years, I have borrowed from the best of these lists. The most influential on my thinking is from Karen A. Mingst and Ivan M. Arreguín-Toft, *Essentials of International Relations*, 7th edition (New York: W. W. Norton, 2016).

[2] I would highly recommend that you actually engage in this exercise, whether your professor requires it or not. This list could simply include bullet points for each attribute and how each theory addresses the key question. But by completing this exercise, you will have a comparative chart (a cheat sheet of sorts) to reference as you apply these theories to the rest of the semester's content.

[3] Tim Dunne, Lene Hansen, and Colin Wight, "The End of International Relations Theory," *The European Journal of International Relations*, 19 no. 3 (2013): 415–17.

[4] Dunne, Hansen, and Wight, "The End of International Relations Theory," 416.

Works Cited

Dunne, Tim, Lene Hansen, and Colin Wight. 2013. "The End of International Relations Theory." *The European Journal of International Relations*. 19 no. 3: 405–25.

Mingst, Karen A., and Ivan M. Arreguín-Toft. 2016. *Essentials of International Relations*, 7th edition. New York: W. W. Norton.

Index

About the Contributors

Alice D. Ba is a professor of political science and international relations (IR) at the University of Delaware. Her research considers the IR of Southeast Asia with a focus on the Association of Southeast Asian Nations (ASEAN), its relations with the United States and China, and the institutional dimensions of a changing regional order. The author of *(Re)Negotiating East and Southeast Asia: Region, Regionalism, and the Association of Southeast Asian Nations* (Stanford 2009), she serves on several editorial boards and has received U.S. Fulbright awards for her work in Beijing and Singapore.

Matthew J. Hoffmann is a professor in the Department of Political Science at the University of Toronto, Scarborough. He is also codirector of the Environmental Governance Lab at the Munk School of Global Affairs. Professor Hoffmann's research and teaching interests include global governance, climate change politics, and IR theory.

Mark Sachleben is a professor of political science at Shippensburg University in Shippensburg, Pennsylvania. He teaches classes in IR, international law and organization, global governance, and human rights. He organizes and leads short-term study abroad experiences to Europe and the Caribbean as well. His current research interest focuses on transnational issues and nontraditional security threats. Among his recent publications is *World Politics on Screen: Understanding International Relations through Popular Culture* (2014). Dr. Sachleben received his PhD from Miami University (Ohio) in 2003.

Rosemary E. Shinko is an assistant professor in the School of International Service at American University. She has published articles and book chapters on sovereignty, ethics, power, identity, and resistance practices. She is an IR theorist who characterizes her approach as postmodern/poststructural.

Laura Sjoberg is associate professor of political science at the University of Florida. She holds a BA from the University of Chicago, a JD from Boston College, and PhD in IR from the University of Southern California. Dr. Sjoberg's work has been published in more than three dozen journals in political science, law, IR, gender studies, and geography. She is author or editor of ten books, including, most recently, *Gender, War, and Conflict* (2014) and *Beyond Mothers, Monsters, Whores* (with Caron Gentry, 2015). Her recent projects include an edited volume on quantitative methods in critical and constructivist IR, *Interpretive Quantification* (with J. Samuel Barkin, 2017), and a book on women's perpetration of conflict sexual violence, *Women as Wartime Rapists*, 2016.

About the Editor

Eric K. Leonard is Henkel Family Chair in International Affairs and Professor of Political Science at Shenandoah University. Dr. Leonard's passion is teaching. He has been teaching in higher education for twenty years and has taught a wide array of courses, including survey courses in international relations, comparative politics, and American government, along with upper-level courses in U.S. foreign policy, political philosophy, and human rights. His research focuses on humanitarian law and its implementation and impact on the current global order. He is the author of *The Onset of Global Governance: International Relations Theory and the International Criminal Court*, along with several articles and case studies on humanitarian law, U.S. foreign policy, and global governance.